GET YOUR GODDESS ON

Own Your Power * Love Your Life!

---

*April —
Love your Goddess
with All your
Heart!
♡ Cat*

What people are saying about GET YOUR GODDESS ON

The layers of potent truth in this book matched with Cat's fabulous humor is by far one of the greatest treats I've had in my lifetime. This book sweetens the journey!

— **Jo Standing | President of the Viva Standing Foundation and author of *Conquer Trauma Drama: Get Your Life***

No matter where you are in your life—you will benefit from this enlightening read.

— **Roxy Holiday | Artist and resident redhead**

This beautifully written book whispers to your soul throughout, likenesses in all of our paths as women, helping us gently renew that spark within and awaken that part of us that is meant to shine and a subtle reminder that each of us is growing through something in our past. Thank you, Cat, for reminding us that we are all goddesses.

— **Ulli Bufton | Business owner and property manager**

This book is phenomenal with its excellent tools to help all people grow and get "unstuck" from the merry go round of life!

— **Sheila Wooding | Mother and grandmother**

We tend to cleanse our physical bodies on a regular basis—hoping that each time the effects would be the impetus to change. Get Your Goddess On focuses on and helps you cleanse your spiritual being. It's gentle, progressive, thought provoking process is a gift for women of any age. The only prescription I will have by my bedside!

— **Elizabeth (Tipi) Borges | Nonprofit project manager and development director**

This book is a revolutionary experience that everyone needs to be a part of to heal themselves and their lives. How cool it is to be able to take back the inner power they never knew they had.

— **Alexi Moles | Licensed massage therapist**

This helped my find answers I've been searching for. Being so congenial and giving my power away constantly made me expect from others what I denied myself: LOVE and acceptance. Now I know that I can be the person I really always wanted to be in my perfect imperfection. Thank you.

— **Waltraud Wascher | Language trainer**

GET YOUR GODDESS ON

Own Your Power * Love Your Life!

CAT DOLS

Blue Bookshelf Publishing
Cedarburg, WI

©Copyright 2017 Catherine M. Dols

DISCLAIMER

The information in this book is provided for informational purposes only and is not a substitute for professional medical advice. The author and publisher make no legal claims, express or implied, and the material is not intended to replace the services of a physician.

The author, publisher and/or copyright holder assume no responsibility for the loss or damage caused, or allegedly caused, directly or indirectly by the use of information contained in this book. The author and publisher specifically disclaim any liability incurred from the use or application of the contents of this book.

All rights reserved. No part of this book may be reproduced or transmitted in any form by any means, electronic, mechanical, photocopying, recording or otherwise, without the prior written permission of the publisher.

The scanning, uploading, and distribution of this book via the Internet or via any other means without the permission of the publisher is illegal and punishable by law.

Any resemblance of any names or characters, businesses or places, events or incidents to actual persons, living or dead or actual events, is purely coincidental and is simply from the perspective and opinion of the author.

Printed in the United States of America
First printing: May 2017
ISBN 978-0-9986915-7-2
Library of Congress Control Number 2017904468
Blue Bookshelf Publishing, Cedarburg, WI

Photo Credits, front cover and author photographs, Katy Rowe,
   www.artistgroup.net
Cover design by Deana Riddle, BookStarter.com
Editing by Heidi Grauel, The Grauel Group

TABLE OF CONTENTS

Acknowledgments	ix
Preface A Journey of Life, Love and Healing	xi
Chapter 1 Look in the Mirror: Who Do You See?	1
Chapter 2 Finding Your Goddess	15
Chapter 3 The Stories We Tell	27
Chapter 4 How to Stop Miss Congeniality	43
Chapter 5 Mistakes and Lessons	73
Chapter 6 The Avoidance Zone	85
Chapter 7 The Story of My Forgiveness	101
Chapter 8 Authentic Goddess Relationships	133
Chapter 9 Get Your Power Back	165
Chapter 10 The Power of Choice	183
Chapter 11 How to Get What You Want	213
Chapter 12 Now that Your Goddess Is On	235
Chapter 13 Supportive Resources	245
Chapter 14 Goddess Book Club Guide	263
About the Author	267

ACKNOWLEDGMENTS

I am grateful to many who assisted me on my journey to discover my Goddess.

To all those who have taught me lessons, both dreaded and desired. I am stronger because of you and for what you have inspired in me.

To the literary agent from New York who told me that I had no business writing a book. Your words both crushed me and lit a fire within, which continues to burn brightly.

To my Quantum Leap team who held my hand as I toddled through this learning process: Steve Harrison, Trish Troilo, Geoffrey Berwind, Gail Snyder, Mary Giuseffi, Raia King, and the beloved Martha Bullen who has the patience of a saint.

To my generous author friends Michael Dow, Terri Britt, and Jo Standing for answering endless questions I didn't even know I needed to ask.

To my Sister Goddess beta readers who gave me honest feedback and clarity as they reminded me to keep my day job for now: Alexi, Brooke, Deb, Elaine, Ginny, Janice, Jo, Katy, Kristina, Pat, Peggy, Sheila, Terri, Tipi, Ulrike, and Waltraud.

Get Your Goddess On!

To my design team who did things I could not do: Lilly for computer stuff, website and social media, to Katy for your fabulous photos and for listening when I needed you. oxox

To my editor Heidi for your expertise and ability to make sense of all my words and run on sentences.

To Deana for your cover design, your abilities beyond the scope of my comprehension, and your patience.

To my mom Pat; my children Brant, Justin, Alexandria, and Veronica; My grand-boys Grant and Taylor; and my furry boys Mr. Woochie and Dexter. You are my rocks and my favorite reasons to wake up happy every day.

I also share my grace and peace with my sweet inner child, My authentic Goddess and You, God. Without you, the journey would be meaningless.

PREFACE

A Journey of Life, Love, and Healing

If you're like me, you sometimes check in with yourself about key milestones or challenges in your life. Finances, where to live, what you can afford, items on your bucket list, and what direction you want your career to go in are all what I call "external life checks" that can be listed, measured, and are really more like goals.

As a decorator, stager, and life coach, I have assisted many people with their goals by assessing their homes to sell or revamping their existing space. I have also done many "internal life checks" with clients, discussing the way they want to live, as well as the quality of their lives. In both these processes, we have reinvented ideas and concepts, replaced what doesn't work with what does, and restaged the most fundamental parts of my clients' inner and outer living spaces. The purpose was to make their lives more meaningful.

What we are doing together in this book is assessing your life so that you can own your personal power and allow yourself to truly love your life again. The probability of your life improving and learning memorable lessons on your journey is great.

I bet I can relate to you. In fact, I could be you. I grocery shop in leggings, a sweatshirt, and no makeup. I am a mom, sister, daughter, friend, and chauffeur. I volunteer at school and the local movie theater. I am divorced, have an associate degree, no celebrity status, work for a living, and can embarrass my teenager by simply existing.

Get Your Goddess On!

Now that I've climbed out of the deep trenches of life, my experiences have helped me formulate a spectacular message for other women. Think of this as a step-by-step healing journey toward the power within that I call a Goddess. It's time to create awareness to know that she exists and discover how to fully access her, to live an authentic life, and experience the love and joy we all deserve.

Goddess is a lofty name for a profound space inside each of us. I use this term to represent my inner connection to my true self, because it honors both my higher power and my inner power at the same time. To own this concept and actually get your Goddess on, you'll find amazingly positive ways to treat yourself with respect and compassion.

That long and winding path to reconnect with my authentic self surprisingly led me to a transformation to a new me. The most important thing I discovered is that **I am already enough** and **I actually matter in the world!** These are two things that I had never owned about myself and soon realized that I wasn't the only woman to have lived with a "less than" attitude in life. I treated myself like I didn't matter; no wonder I gave others permission to do the same thing. Not anymore.

At the beginning of any journey, there are usually preparations we make to ensure a successful experience along the way. What we take with us are usually things that might be helpful on our trip. Because this is also the abbreviated version of my journey, hindsight lends a hand in selecting what is best to bring along. Here are the things I recommend bringing along on our trip together: a sense of infinite possibility; an openness to introspection, change, and responsibility; and a willingness to love yourself as you embrace your personal power.

A Journey of Life, Love, and Healing

By giving our power away, we have played the victim, second guessed ourselves, and felt worthless. By being passionate about all the lessons we learned in the trial and error process called life, it can help us to regain our power while on our Goddess path. How many women are searching for the power they gave away? This series of my learned lessons is actually a personal invitation to all women to truly know and love yourselves again. Be grateful that you are on this journey to discover you. Imagine what it would be like if we all brought that authentic level of trust, love, and support to every part of our lives . . . oh, how the world would change. I trust that together, we can make a difference in raising the consciousness of authenticity by sharing it with those around us.

My wish for you all is to please write in your book, make notes, participate in the questions at the end of each chapter, and highlight the parts that speak to you. Play in the process, be the process, enjoy the process! Get in your comfy clothes and grab your favorite blanket and beverage; it's time to Get Your Goddess On! Let's begin the conversation . . .

CHAPTER ONE

Look in the Mirror: Who Do You See?

> Who you think you are is not always who you are to the world. If you camouflage anything about yourself, then you are pretending. There is nothing authentic about pretending and it will stop you from owning your power and knowing your Goddess.

Time to Start the Party

I love to go to parties as much as I love to plan them. With all events, there are preparations to be made. It's important to know what the theme is, as well as who is coming, the menu, an itinerary, and of course who is the guest of honor. Everyone loves to help with all the fun stuff, but no one really likes to do the clean up before or after the party. Unfortunately, it's necessary for any party's success, so we have to do it. Let's look at what your life party will be all about.

Get Your Goddess On!

Your theme is your power, you are showing up for you, and I am helping you with your preparations. Your menu has responsibility, authenticity, gratitude, and forgiveness as the main entrées, with side dishes of stories, mistakes, and choices to snack on as well. Your itinerary is fourteen chapters of a journey that starts when you begin reading and ends when you love your Goddess. The party is for you, by you, and all about you.

With any party, we know that the fun will eventually happen, so let's address the part no one really wants to deal with: the cleaning up time before our party begins. The first several chapters are your cleansing process. Not as much fun as the later chapters, but extremely important for the success of your party. In fact, the thoroughness of your pre-party cleaning has a direct correlation as to how well your party turns out. For efficiency's sake, our post-party clean-up will be done along the way, in the questions at the end of each chapter.

Cleansing your life is a little like doing a healing cleanse to rid your body of toxins. You can do it slowly over a period of weeks or quickly in a matter of days. At times, it can feel very uncomfortable when things come up that you don't want to deal with. Please stay with your experience, knowing that the rewards at the end will all be worth it.

Create a Space for Your Goddess

Are you ready to discover your inner Goddess power and live an authentic life? Even if you don't think you are ready for a change, I ask you to open yourself up to live in possibility for the duration of our time together.

Look in the Mirror: Who Do You See?

The very best place to begin is to quiet your mind, be still, and externally create a space filled with beauty and peace. At first, it is best that you practice mindfully in this safe and quiet place—later you will be able to do this anywhere. If your life is complicated and everything else seems to be more important than you are, then it's time to shift and become your own #1 priority.
Look at your schedule, your life, and your daily routine. Prioritize.

Take two, three, or more things out; delegate or say no to everything that is not totally necessary as often as possible. Practice saying no in the mirror first, then role play with a friend if you are addicted to saying yes to everyone and everything. You will know when you have shifted.

Now, think about your car. You take care of your car because you rely on it. You wouldn't run your car without gas and oil, would you? You regularly recharge and refuel your car as often as needed. This is what is necessary to do for yourself as well. Think of you, take care of you, and recharge as often as you need to, because you have to rely on yourself 100%. You matter, so start treating yourself that way.

Take a Look Inside . . .

*BE Close your eyes and listen to yourself breathe. Create your atmosphere . . . If you like candles, a bubble bath, or sitting on a beach, arrange to be alone in that space. Choose to be filled with joy and peace while you are there. At first, this will mean that if you are playing soccer mom for the weekend tournament, find another time. With practice, it will become second nature and eventually will be your connection to your Goddess power and you will be able to access this space anywhere, anytime. Also, be in a state of gratitude as you breathe.

Get Your Goddess On!

*BE STILL Quiet yourself and quiet your mind by relaxing, meditating, breathing deeply, and loving yourself. Repeat regularly. Appreciate who you are and be proud of the difference your existence makes in the world.

*BELIEVE this is possible. Believe there's a part of you that is a Goddess, a power center of strength, love, and light. Trust this state of mind. If this is difficult for you, start with simply wanting it to be true, then move into believing. When you hear distracting voices in your head that could be your ego or fear, ask those voices to step aside.

*TAKE A SELF-ASSESSMENT by either actually standing or sitting in front of a mirror or having a pad of paper with you and a virtual mirror in your head as you sit in your peaceful place. Ask yourself several questions that can help you identify where you are presently. The tough ones are crucial for progress. Start by honestly answering these:

> *Who am I?*
> *Who am I pretending to be?*
> *Am I in a safe place?*
> *Am I worthy to receive goodness in my life?*
> *Describe my ideal self.*
> *Describe what my perfect life looks like.*
> *What in my life is serving my highest good?*
> *What are my emotional and physical assets?*
> *What brings me joy?*
> *What is my favorite word to describe myself?*
> *How am I in service to the world?*
> *Am I authentic? In what ways?*
> *Do I support myself in my life?*
> *How do I define what my Goddess is?*
> *Where did I leave my power?*

Look in the Mirror: Who Do You See?

When do I feel less than?
When do I feel absolutely fantastic?
What areas of my life am I proud of?
How can I be more balanced and set healthy boundaries?

By answering honestly, you create the building blocks to begin your path back to your Goddess. Some of you may already feel that this power is with you immediately; some may need to do more clearing and searching to discover where you stashed her away long ago.

Everyone starts from where they are. It took you years to get where you are right now, so cut yourself some slack in this discovery process! Clarity in various stages will occur along your path. All I ask is that you have faith in you and allow yourself to receive the joy of this cleansing process. This means you have to stop any and all pretending.

My Favorite Pity Party

I was once driving home from a meeting and my passenger was a divorced woman who didn't know she was pretending who she was to the world. After eight years, she was still having a giant pity party about her husband having an affair that eventually dissolved their marriage. I asked her to tell me her story of the demise. When she started with blame immediately, I stopped her and asked her to tell me her story from a first-person point of view.

She was silent for a few miles, visibly angry at me for having the audacity to think she had anything to do with it! (I was actually thinking my timing was bad also, since I still had an hour to drive with her and had no way to escape.) She was frustrated with me for even suggesting it, but she began. I heard some things in her story that prompted me to ask a couple questions.

Get Your Goddess On!

I asked her questions that gave her the opportunity for an epiphany that she had longed for but didn't know existed. My questions were, "Where were you when this affair was going on?" and "How were you being in your marriage at that time?" She was silent, then she cried and confessed that she had never, ever thought of this before. She had been a mom, a teacher, a volunteer, a friend, a sister, a daughter/caretaker to elderly parents, and sometimes a wife. She really wasn't there for him at all and hadn't felt a connection with him in the last few years of their marriage while the affair had been going on. She had enjoyed being everything else but a wife, but still loved the title. She knew they had grown apart, yet was still putting up a good front for social events. I believe this is the definition of pretending.

She talked, cried, screamed a little, and then did the unthinkable: as we pulled into her driveway, she called her ex-husband to apologize for being absent in the last part of their marriage. Yes, she did! And he actually thanked her! She took back her power at that moment.

What an hour can do, by adding some soul searching, being in a confined space with a life coach, and finally being ready and willing to release. . . . Sometimes it's unbelievable that we can carry things for years, then let them go in an instant!

Did it change the fact that he screwed around on her? No. Was he still wrong for doing so? Absolutely yes. Did it change the fact that she mentally checked out of their marriage long before the affair? No. Do two wrongs make a right? No, just two wrongs. But she was able to acknowledge her own actions, take responsibility, then she was able to easily release her anger and resentment.

She got the freedom that she didn't know was possible and they ended up getting along as divorced parents far better afterward.

It did not change what happened, just how she looked at it. What changed the most is that she finally took back her power.

> *When you stay in blame, your power stays with the other person. It's one of the amazing places we lose ourselves because we have willingly given our power away with the blame. When you do this, you get farther from your Goddess.*

Stop pretending, because you are fooling no one and hurting yourself.

A Place of Responsibility

You will never get anywhere unless you start to take full responsibility for all of you. Your life results can be measured, appreciated, cursed, loved, and used as excuses, motivators, or learning tools. As you were answering your questions, did you notice any repetition in your answers? If so, you now have found where you can begin to take responsibility.

I spent quite a few years in denial, frustration, anger, and blame with a few similar characteristics that showed up in my less-than-stellar relationships. I was a great hostess to my own pity party, until I finally took absolute responsibility for those results. Before that, I had been held captive, felt like a failure, and had given most of my power away. No wonder both my marriages went bad even though I felt like I was a being such a nice person. (That's actually what the problem was and how I became such a victim, but I didn't realize that.) Why had this happened and why didn't anyone come to rescue me?

The answers came later, from years of soul searching and with parts of books and courses of self-discovery to help me look within. I had

Get Your Goddess On!

to force myself to listen, learn, and be open to the truth because I was so sick of getting less-than results. I may have asked myself those tough questions earlier in my life, but I didn't answer them honestly until I was in my forties. It was finally time to look within and own all of me, including my behavior.

I already knew exactly what my exes had done to create the divorces after running those blaming scenarios over and over in my head. I knew all too well the times when they were less than wonderful to me, making some monumental contributions to the demise of our marriages. Now it was time to tell the same story on the same stage, but this time I was the star of the responsibility/blame show.

What could I have done to create the horrible results I had gotten as I became the super victim? Could I have done something without realizing it? Yes. I was staring at two broken marriages on that stage and I was one of the lead characters in the cast of both shows. When I reached over and took off my victim mask, to clear my vision, I sat and thought. The only way I could see my truth and get off the blame train was to do what I just asked you to do: a self-assessment. I was overcome with gratitude when the truth finally surfaced.

I eventually faced myself in my virtual mirror and what came up changed my life! I told my sad divorce "woe is me" story out loud, to the audience in the mirror. *Then*, reluctantly, I told it again, this time from a place of responsibility. I told it in first person: "I created my divorce the first time by _____, and then did it again for my second one."

Not my proudest moments for either of my divorces, but it really felt amazing to work through all the extra baggage. It might take a couple of attempts (read, several), but please do this exercise for yourself, by yourself, and in your safe space. No one will ever hear or see you do this, unless you want them to. The first couple run-throughs really suck, literally! Nasty stuff comes up and that place where you keep your stress in your body might just get a little wild. Then there is that moment: You can actually feel it in your heart when you "get" what your part in the play was! The honest and authentic truths that show up in this process are crucial to your success and your breakthroughs to your Goddess. Realize how important it is to show up for yourself in this exercise. Without being fully present, it becomes just some story. By showing up 100%, it could be your ticket to freedom—it definitely was for me. Did I want to take responsibility? No, not at first, but now, I can't imagine living any other way.

Miss Congeniality Takes the Banner Off

So, what were my results with my virtual mirror, my epiphany, and my moment of truth? Here it is: the realization that I was really good at being Miss Congeniality . . . for a while. That last part was the key to my whole undoing! I had been unhappy in my first marriage and after we grew farther apart and worked through years of salvaging effort, I left when I realized it was past fixing.

I got involved with husband #2 so quickly I didn't have time to thoroughly think things through. I must have been looking for some sort of validation for myself. What I really needed was validation from *within* myself, not from someone else. It was all too much too soon and I got swept away without knowing who he really was, so it was doomed from the start. Being too congenial, especially in the beginning, was still my way of being, so I sunk back into my familiar role again, until it eventually started to wear on me.

Was I in love? Yes, I truly believed I was both times. I was miscued though, because I really was still just in my excessive people-pleasing mode. So not much was really real in either of my marriages and pretending was the only way I knew how to be in a relationship at that time.

One strange thing about both husbands is that I don't remember either man ever really telling me the truth about why they wanted to marry me. If they would have, I'm guessing it was because I was so easy to get along with in the beginning—sad reason. I promised myself to be smarter if I ever think about getting married again.

I might just ask him to read this book first before we decide to get involved, so he knows ahead of time that I am retired from being too nice all the time. I can visualize it now: If I see some potential on our first date, picture me pulling out my book and telling him that he will possibly get a second date, if he still wants one, when he's done reading it. Too funny!

Looking back to earlier installments of my relationship movies, I think I had been thrilled that many guys had been interested in me. I was impressed at their gestures as they courted me and I ended up falling in "pretend" love with them because of their sweet talk, trips, and vast promises. Even though I didn't really know how to love, it unfortunately didn't stop me from signing up for the whole package more than once.

I also remember making sure that I didn't lose them. I went along with everything they wanted for quite a while and as long as I had become everything they wanted me to be, all was good! I had to be really interested in what they wanted to do, so I continued to be the living, breathing, sad version of Miss Congeniality, with the car, house, and the hot tub out back. And here's the clincher... Ready? ... This is going to be a shocker... they really liked it! Unfortunately, I didn't because my overly people-pleasing state of mind usually left me feeling very empty inside. Hindsight showed me that because it felt meaningless, as soon as this behavior became a chore, I lost my desire to continue, so it ultimately didn't last forever!

Look in the Mirror: Who Do You See?

When I started to take my banner off, to change into a more real, authentic, and less sparkly version of the real Cat, the magic was gone with the sparkles. And I realized that even though I had grown to love both husbands over the years, I didn't *really* like them—at all. I really didn't like some of the things they liked to do, or who they were, who they had become, or who I had become with them, banner on or off. I felt resentful toward them, not realizing that I was the one who was being overly congenial. I also didn't *get* that I had any responsibility, because they were treating me in a lesser way and I was the victim. It never occurred to me that I had given my permission.

Each time I had found my voice, the relationships fell apart. The saddest part is that with my behavior, I had taught them that it was okay to treat me in a way that focused on only what they wanted and not what mattered to me. I had willingly given away too much of my power in many of my relationships, without thinking through the consequences of my actions.

By taking responsibility, it was also a giant step in the direction of authenticity! In fact, I had a ton to do with the demise of my relationships! I had actually unknowingly begun the demise before the marriages even started, so there was *no* possible chance of success.

This represents one of my major stages of healing, when I started to take on 100% of my responsibility in my failed relationships. At first, nothing about this was easy to swallow. It did, however, create the atmosphere where I was finally able to see what I had done and, interestingly, my consequences were in direct correlation with my actions!

I had unknowingly sabotaged myself, directly affecting the outcome of my failed marriages. Garbage in, garbage out, as they say. This was not fun to realize, but necessary for my own personal

Get Your Goddess On!

transformation into my authentic self. The more power I regained during this discovery process, the more I unearthed my Goddess within.

By admitting my mistakes, was I, in any way, deleting any contributions that my exes made to the divorces? Absolutely not. It did bring me the best gift in the world: clarity! And it brought me to *me*! Telling each of the stories of my failed relationships in first-person responsibility mode was one of the best things I've ever done and was one of my first official freedom stops off the blame train. When I owned it, I could finally release the hold my painful lessons had on me and was able take back my power!

The most important key to living life in a new way, without repeating the same mistakes, is to learn and remember the lesson. Did it take only one session in the mirror? No, several, because I had layers and years of stories I had piled on top of each other to own up to.

Being too nice for that many years meant that I had a closet full of lovely gowns! (Think about the *27 Dresses* movie scene when she cleans out that amazing closet of bridesmaid dresses!) Give yourself permission to peel the layers back. When you release in layers and stages, sometimes it works better. Other times, trust me, go for the quick-release Band Aid method!

With my new realizations, I vowed to rewrite the sequels of my own movie marathon and be a smart writer this time. It was an eye-opening time in my life, and I finally found the courage to love and take responsibility for the real me. Not who I wanted to be, not who I pretended to be, just me! I also became very grateful for the opportunities my true voice brought forth.

My mother ended up surprising me with some beautifully authentic relationship encouragement in a roundabout way. She met and

Look in the Mirror: Who Do You See?

married the love of her life at the tender age of 75. By doing so, she confirmed that there is truly hope for me yet! There is still time to get it right, by being authentic and attracting that same type of person in a healthy relationship.

The rest of my story is that I chose to abstain from dating for years, as my happily self-induced consequence to get clarity, to build my business, write a book, and just enjoy being a woman and a mom. I really got to know myself 100% and I ended up finally liking the person I had become—*tons* better than the old me! By spending time as just me, I was able to discover my Goddess with countless moments of reflection, often by regularly looking at myself and my behavior. Polish up that virtual mirror and as you gaze upon that phenomenal Goddess, make friends with her. I believe that when you get to know her, you will really love her.

Taking full responsibility for your thoughts, actions, and behavior is not always fun, but it's a necessary part of our party clean-up process that has to be done. Your Goddess sure doesn't want to be a part of the blame, shame, resentment game, and neither do your party guests (aka the people in your life). Introspection into the parts of your life that you don't want to look at gets easier when you start to answer accountably. The sooner your space is ready, the sooner your Goddess and your guests will arrive.

Chapter 1 Questions

1. If you haven't done the self-assessment exercise yet, please do it now. Write in the spaces after each question. Reflect here what your major results are.

   _____

   _____

Get Your Goddess On!

2. Tell your own pity party story in your usual way. Then tell the same story in the first-person responsibility mode. How did your story change? Describe how you feel about those changes and what your responsibility is in the second version of the story.

CHAPTER TWO

Finding Your Goddess

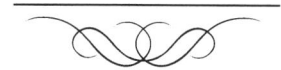

> "We are not human beings going through a spiritual experience, we are spiritual beings going through a human experience." —Author unknown (but very smart)

Your Goddess is a part of your original divine light, your authentic soul. The piece of you that has always been there, before your physical body was born, and will be there long after you are gone from here. When you operate from this place of who you are at your core, it is very powerful.

I define Goddess as the place of power inside each of us that gives us the confidence in knowing who we are and how we fit into the world. This inner compass also emanates love, positive energy, authenticity, accountability, kindness, and the desire to make a profound difference in life.

The True Meaning of Goddess

We are here to discuss the Goddess that is *you*, the true *you*. Keep reminding yourself that your authentic core is who your Goddess is. What she is is everything you already want to be and is perfectly you. Remember, this is unlimited power if you are willing to unearth her from the space where she's been stuffed away.

Those of you who already own and rock your inner Goddess: this is an opportunity to embrace her even more and feel the confidence of confirmation that you are already on the sweet Goddess path of life. Be grateful for knowing and loving your Goddess power already.

The secret of this entire book is to let you know that you already have everything inside that you need to be complete—whether you believe it or not.

Every person, no matter what age, size, color, religion, nationality, or sexual preference, is just waiting to be acknowledged. You may have forgotten who you are, denied yourself love and respect, or didn't know that your Goddess existed, but she is there. My wish for you is that you not only recognize yourself again, but also embrace your Goddess, love her, then introduce her to the world!

It is *your* Goddess, your journey, and your possibilities. Own yourself and your Goddess and get ready to live a whole new way again. Yes again, I have already eluded to the fact that you knew her before you lost her. You knew her when you were that amazing little child full of life and possibility. The world was at your fingertips, and you felt that you could do absolutely anything!

Goddess energy is like the unconditional love of a child, the real deal. It is contagious and enlightening, speaking volumes without words. She is also aligned with you, herself, your higher power, and

Finding Your Goddess

the universe all at the same time! This multifaceted connection is amazingly abundant and was born out of unconditional love.

I had originally perceived this place to be far bigger, better, and more wonderful than myself. What I didn't realize is that it's actually a part of me, not bigger than me. Having been through my share of adversity, I found other women who were going through similar life issues and were also searching for healing. Since I wasn't the only one down in those trenches, I discovered that sharing my knowledge was beneficial for both of us.

Have you ever closed yourself off from the world emotionally, felt destroyed, defeated, and worthless as a result of the challenges in your life? I did, because of how I was avoiding dealing with those challenges. I was on total overload. I realized that no one was going to magically heal me, get my power back for me, or automatically download some new awareness while I was sleeping. It would require dedicated action on my part, darn it. One of the keys to recovery was to actively participate in my own search for healing. This was originally a very unwelcomed idea, until I became grateful for the vast amount of value gained from being 100% involved.

Your Goddess Journey Begins

Why do we define ourselves by our circumstances or other people's comments and judgments? It seems to me that almost every woman has reasons as to why they aren't enough, generally stemming from something someone else said to them or their own negative self-talk. Nothing could be farther from the truth.

Every woman is an authentic Goddess whether she knows it or admits it or not. It's time that each of us realize our own truth and give our hearts permission to love ourselves fully. It's also time to

Get Your Goddess On!

begin by becoming aware of our place of power that has been sitting dormant for a very long time.

Awareness is about paying attention and putting the puzzle pieces together. Being aware of who we truly are is being authentic. There's no way we can expect to have authenticity just show up in our lives without first being authentic ourselves. The opposite of authenticity is being fake, selfish, and ego-driven. There is absolutely no room for your ego when you have your Goddess on! You have a choice to live in personal power or in ego, but not both. In fact, your ego can take that well-deserved permanent vacation. Bon Voyage!

> *Here's my secret to being aware of the origin of my Goddess: I believe her to be a little piece of God that he put inside me as my soul was being created. It's the part that connects me with Him as my higher power at all times. I just forgot it was there for a really long time.*

I'd like to clarify that I believe in a higher power that I refer to as God. I also believe this higher power can be perceived to be male or female and look vastly different to many people. For the sake of popularity, I refer to God as a male figure in this book. If you have a different belief, please insert your personal title for your power source as you read. Make this your own.

I am advocating that the Age of Awareness goes side by side with the Age of Technology that is currently bombarding us in every aspect of life. What if we spent as much time internally speaking the truth about who we are and how we are in the world, as we do playing with technology on our computers and phones? The world would be a better place. We can't do anything about something that we don't know exists, so awareness is the first key.

It is also immensely comforting to consciously be aware of how connected we are with every person on the planet, as well as to our higher power and ourselves. Once we internalize this connection and become aware of the bigger picture we are a part of, life shifts to a place of love and compassion for the world. It's one of the many stops on our journey to find our Goddess. Be grateful for the connectedness, compassion, and for all our similarities as well as our differences. Without uniqueness in the world, it would be a pretty boring place.

The Misleading Word Association

Another part our journey involves stumbling blocks in our path. One of those is the misuse of the term Sex Goddess, which has done plenty of damage to objectify women in society. When the words sex and goddess are used together, they usually involve pretty lofty criteria, referring to a type of physical beauty that is unattainable for most women. We unfortunately see many women sadly getting lost in this objectifying process. By focusing all of their resources, time, and ambition in search of this outer beauty, it becomes a trap, blowing us off course from living an authentic life.

This over-used combination of sex and goddess is why most of us regular women may find it difficult to imagine we have a Goddess within us. I invite you to realize that these are just two words someone put together. Traditionally, Goddesses in history and mythology have been held in places of high honor and reverence. I choose to embrace that vision instead.

Let's also keep in mind that these modern-day sex goddesses are also daughters, sisters, wives, and sometimes moms. They are just as vulnerable as we are. I wonder what insight Marilyn Monroe could have offered us if she were still alive. I think beneath the makeup, the sex symbol act, and all the glamor, she was someone

Get Your Goddess On!

I would have liked. I'll bet she was just a girl who wanted to make a difference in the world too, but she didn't quite know how. I'm curious what she truly wished for and how she would look at the world now. I wonder if she would have made the same choices today, based on the awareness we now have available.

Being sensual and sexual are also definitely part your inner power, and owning them in a healthy way is crucial. When we treat our sexual energy as a gift and an asset, it becomes a positive attribute that can enhance our true essence. By living in the truth of our sexuality, we are being authentically true to ourselves and in our relationships. Honesty is the key.

Two other very common titles in society that are paired with Goddess are domestic and garden and can probably help you visualize this concept. I was a Domestic Goddess for 20 years and made a big difference for my family in that role. I have also been a Garden Goddess for 40+ years because it's an activity that I can get as dirty as I want and end up with a beautiful space when I'm done! The familiar Garden and Domestic Goddess titles might relate closer to your life—it definitely helped me grasp the concept as I was beginning my journey.

Goddess and the Law of Attraction

We really are a product of our thoughts. Goddess energy finds other Goddess energy. It has been scientifically proven that we are all made of energy and the vibrational energy of a person aligns with the vibrational energy of what they think about. So, we can actually create what we think about as demonstrated in the popular book and movie The Secret, which is all about the law of attraction. Since we have a choice as to what we attract into our lives, why not use it to our advantage?

That's how we can create the circumstances and expectations of how people show up in our lives. You can manifest them as either whole and authentic, or manipulative and damaged, depending on our own focus at that time. In other words, those things we want to receive show up for us in direct correlation to how we are being. For example, if we are angry and frustrated, other people and situations will show up angry and frustrated in our lives because it mirrors and supports our way of being with the same vibrational energy.

It works the same when we are being loving, generous, and kind, since we are able to receive things like abundance, joy, love, and prosperity at all times. You can choose the way you want your life to be by knowing this information. Too bad I didn't actually know it was an option for most of my life, but now I can imagine the great things I dream about and have the life I actually want!

Goddess Looks

Outside is easy and can be as immaterial as you choose it to be. Your Goddess can look like every kind of woman on the outside and is beyond any specific physical attributes. We can also see qualities like being courageous, strong, generous, selfless, tenacious, brave, fearless, loving, and grateful, because it has become that woman's way of being. Other people can tell when a woman is comfortable in her own skin and they feel good when they are around her. That's what a Goddess looks like.

Internal beauty shining through can also be a byproduct of living and connecting with yourself beyond the chains of ego and fears. It's time to put aside whatever level of importance on the outside for now and focus on our healthy, loving, and powerful inside.

Conflicting Thoughts on Goddess

I'd venture that possibly half of the women who pick up this book have questions, doubts, or conflicting thoughts about this Goddess concept of power and strength. Most women believe in the popular women's or mothers' intuition as an internal and unexplainable power. This is definitely part of your Goddess too, but with a new twist: we can also access this power to change our lives. I know this is possible because I did it.

If you are so far away from this way of thinking that you can't even spell Goddess, it's okay, I couldn't either. I actually had to look the word up as I wrote it for the first time because it didn't look right. I also wasn't 100% sure about many of the words that became key areas of focus like authenticity, responsibility, gratitude, and trust. I ended up looking up all the key words to fully understand their meanings beyond my limited scope of understanding.

The result of my search is in the Supportive Resources chapter in the back of the book, entitled Goddess Glossary. I also created my own definition of each of the words and have left a space for you to define the terms, if you choose. True understanding of key concepts may help you with some of your conflicts along the way. With knowledge and understanding, it will help you to be more open and participate fully in creating your own map of possibilities.

It's also important to address the topic of our internal verbal conflicts called excuses. They are rampant things that can block the creation of your Goddess map. The blockages, or excuses, that come up when you look at what is possible are the things that you tell yourself and others so you can live outside the truth. Excuses are primarily used to hide who you really are. People can eventually tell what you look like no matter who you pretend to be or how good you are at hiding the real you.

The funny thing about excuses is that they only keep you from the truth because others can see through you. In the end, you are a truly magnificent being and by continuously keeping yourself from the truth, you may never really know how phenomenal you are.

When you hear the voice in your head that casts doubt, fear, or anger to create your excuses, ask yourself, where is this coming from? Who is speaking? These are crucial questions. If you ask that voice to quiet and listen to your Goddess, you will find your truth. Give yourself permission to override those misleading voices whenever they come up.

Continue to Clean House

Your pre-party cleanup still continues before your party can begin. It's time to focus on recognizing the obstacles that are blocking you from a relationship between you and your Goddess. The purpose of the next several chapters is for cleansing your space in order for you to recognize her. Giving your power away is one of the best ways to continue to live haphazardly and avoid your Goddess. Here are a few red flags and warning signs to let you know when you have given your power away:

1. Feeling inferior with certain people or situations.

2. Blaming other people and circumstances for your unhappiness.

3. Looking outward for approval from your job, friends, children, spouse, etc.

4. Identifying only with our title to define ourselves, such as, I am a mom, a doctor, etc.

5. Feeling like you are not enough, like you can't do anything right.

6. Making excuses for things in life where you feel inadequate, vulnerable, or fearful.

These are just a few of the methods women use regularly to bury their Goddess deeper within and give their power away. Practice recognizing the signs by answering the Chapter 2 questions. After answering these questions from your heart, you will have given yourself permission to begin a sweet relationship with your Goddess. Be proud of your honesty and your dedication to this wonderful, power within that you are just getting to know. Congratulations.

Chapter 2 Questions

1. Describe a personal situation for each of the above six red flags. What limitations are involved in these powerless situations?

_____
_____
_____
_____
_____
_____
_____
_____
_____
_____

Finding Your Goddess

2. Even if you have to pretend for now, rewrite the above powerless situations now from a powerful, Goddess point of view, as if you didn't have any more limitations. How do you feel about the same situations from a different point of view?

CHAPTER THREE

The Stories We Tell

We are all natural storytellers. Sometimes we nail it and sometimes we bomb.

Stories are a very abundant part of our lives. There are so many to keep track of because, as we create new ones, we still hold onto the old ones. They can also be a place where we give our power away, depending on what stories we tell ourselves and if we choose to believe them or not.

These tales are not something we can physically touch, but if they were, I would imagine they would look like the things in and around our house that we don't even see anymore. When I go to stage a person's property, that's what I see—all the things that the owners are now blind to because they have been there for so long: the stacks of magazines, newspapers, and bills to pay; the dirty clothes hampers; the extra pieces of furniture in the living room because someone was too lazy to take it down to the basement.

Get Your Goddess On!

That's what I think our stories would look like: they are all over the place and clutter our lives. Some serve us well, but most of them are outdated and don't actually matter to us anymore. Oftentimes they serve to keep us stuck in old ways that don't enhance our lives. Time for "out with the old and in with the new" stories now, ones that actually serve you and your life.

If we want to process the experiences of our lives into new stories, we have to get some of that old, useless stuff out of our minds. We create stories to be able to understand and process information internally, as a way to communicate with ourselves and others. We do this consciously and subconsciously every day of our lives. The problem is because of our subjective perceptive abilities, we don't always know which stories are true and which are false, which sometimes causes confusion in our lives. It's time to clarify our stories.

The Top 10 Things I Know About Stories

1. Stories can be true or false.
2. Some stories can be great learning lessons.
3. Stories can be amazingly helpful and also sadly destructive.
4. Other people's stories about us can change us only if we let them.
5. Changing one thing in a story can change the whole story.
6. Stories can be entertaining, scary, funny, or touching.
7. Positive stories are the best ones to tell myself.
8. My favorite stories are ones that make me laugh.
9. A story can be just one single sentence.
10. The most dangerous stories are the ones I tell myself that are not true.

There is a profound responsibility in storytelling. The purpose of any story is about what happens after the story. Is there an emotion that comes up, a lesson learned, or a feeling that remains with the person who experiences the story? The lasting effects can make a difference for the listener.

As a writer, I also love stories because of the lessons I learn when I write them. Usually, I have an objective in mind at the beginning, but sometimes it changes when I've read the end and realize the bigger picture. I love stories because they also make life more interesting.

The stories that threaten my Goddess the most are the untrue ones, called lies. Those stories can create self-doubt, fear, and self-destruction if I choose to believe them. I used to, but not anymore. If I'm ever tempted to go back to my old ways, I ask myself, "What supports me moving forward? Those old lies or the truth?" I also ask my Goddess to keep me in check because I count on her to always have my back and keep my best interests in mind. I'm grateful to be on this loving and authentic team together.

One-sentence Stories

I am a great mom. I hate motherhood. I'm afraid I'll never have time to be a mom.

I really handle money well. I always have money problems.

I am unlovable. I love to be loved. I am a giver. I am a taker.

I am never going to discover what makes me happy. I am a free spirit.

I know things will always be aligned with the stars. I have a great life. My life sucks.

I am doomed to fail in business. I can succeed in any business.

I have failed in marriage twice, why bother to try to love again? I'm ready to love.

I can do it. I can't do it. I matter. I don't matter.

I am an amazing person, and I can be anything I want to be! I am not enough.

What are you telling yourself right now? How many of the stories to do you have going at one time? Know your stories, because chances are you are believing them. Know that you have the ultimate control over what stories you tell and believe yourself. Do you honor yourself with positive stories? If not, it's time to start.

Ask for help by trusting your Goddess, your #1 cheerleader, to help you filter your self-talk/story mechanism to build yourself up instead of tearing yourself down. The good news is that you can change your story in an instant. What is stopping you from creating the life you want for yourself? In each of these cleansing chapters, we are working on identifying your obstacles, the places where you feel stuck, so that you realize what areas need your attention first.

Two Families, Two Stories

Sometimes obstacles are a part of our lives as adults and we have no idea how they got there, until we look back into our childhood. The beginning of that block for us could have been created because we were fooled by other people's stories that they made up about us. This happens quite often as children, because we do not have the cognitive abilities to discern what stories to believe and what not to believe. Because we don't have a higher order of thinking yet, it is possible that we could have altered our lives just by believing someone else's story about us.

A friend told me a story about two neighbors with different approaches to the same task of teaching their daughters how to ride a bike. Both envisioned their little girls riding that shiny new bike, going through similar steps along the way, but with a critical difference in attitude that created two totally different stories.

Story #1 is about the neighbor on the right. As this little girl grew up, she rode scooters, big wheels, and then a small bike with training wheels. Every level brought positive, supportive encouragement from her parents and family. On the little girl's birthday, she got a sweet big girl bike with all the trimmings!

When that moment arrived, the back of the bike was released and she successfully rode alone. This was the result of many years of training and encouragement as she became officially independent. This rite of passage didn't happen overnight, it took years of patience and practice to create. Her journey was also flavored generously with her parents' positive experiences of bike riding, actually setting this little girl up for a successful result from the beginning.

Story #2 is about the neighbor on the left. This mom had a scary bike riding experience growing up. The language of her mom's tentative encouragement was tainted with very fearful, frightening, and unsupportive undertones instead of being positive and supportive—and the little girl bought into some of the fears and gave a little bit of her power to them. Sadly, the stories of the mom's previous experience and fear of bike riding affected the little girl's chances of success.

Her early riding experiences were altered by her mom's influence, making her tentative and less sure of herself on wheels. Without a major positive intervention, she could have been doomed to repeat her mother's fear of bike riding. Is that fair? No, but it happens all the time: someone else's stories can create major influences in our experiences, if we choose to believe them and make them ours, too. Fortunately, it can be undone.

The result for the second little girl had a happy ending because of the positive influence from her whole family and the other neighbors who had successful first bike riding experiences. She learned to ride beautifully despite whatever original, negative influences she had. Mind over matter! Luckily, the little girl chose to allow the positive influences to be more important in the end and avoided creating the same limitation her mother had when she was younger.

The Pretend Conversation

What if in the end, the little girl decided to take her power back by changing the story that her mother had presented to her? What if she actually had adult-like cognitive abilities as a child? Maybe a pretend conversation with her mother could go something like this, "Mom, I really appreciate the nightmare stories of your childhood bike accident that you've shared with me numerous times. I would love for you to stop though, since I don't plan on making your experience mine. I'm actually a pretty good bike rider now and I wish you'd get over it, because it's really messing you up and I want to see you happy."

How many of us may want to say something like that to our parents, or maybe know that we need to hear it ourselves? When someone alters the story of an event for us with their stuff, they will most likely change our outcome, unless we stand up for ourselves and say no thanks. Be the change for yourself with the most honest pretend conversation you can imagine. We can change our view of the story simply by changing the details and our internal dialog. The very best way to predict and then change our future is to create it ourselves.

The Story I Told Myself About My Childhood

I am a living mistake. It's officially in print. In 1958 new mothers were told that if you nursed a baby, you couldn't get pregnant. Ha. Shortly after my young, lactating mother was told by a nurse that lovely myth, she found out she would be having Irish twins (when two children are born within 12 months to the same mother). I was #2. I am living proof that the nurse was misinformed, because eleven and a half months later, I entered the world.

I was in kindergarten when I asked mom why my sister and I were the same age for two weeks every year. At the time, I would've appreciated the sugar-coated version like, "We were so excited to have children that we wanted to have you girls close together so you could grow up to be best friends." Nope, didn't happen. I got the nurse's story instead. The reality is that it is no big deal, and that lots of children are born without planning on their parents' part, but I chose to let it affect my self-esteem for decades.

None of us want to make mistakes. No one wants to be a mistake either. My mom did not realize that telling me the way-above-my-level-of-comprehension version of the story at the age of five would send me into a 50-year search for answers. Do our parents, or us as parents, do this stuff on purpose? No. I believe most parents do the best they know how to do.

Since I know I can, I have chosen to change my beginning, because no one told me that I couldn't change it. Of course, I didn't ask anyone either. I changed my story for me, by adding a little extra love. Here's how it goes . . .

Get Your Goddess On!

I was a gift, born to two loving parents. My arrival kept our little family on their toes. With the influence of a helpful nurse, my parents knew that one child was certainly not enough. I am the second of four kids and I paved the way for the other two. I also think I helped my mom learn how to multitask at an early age—she became very good at it. I know I was loved from the beginning, because everyone loves gifts.

Same ingredients with a different flavor. I did this because now, as a parent myself, I actually understood the whole story. Young parents, misinformed, shocked at first, loved whoever came, kids grew up, did the best they could, end of story. Here's the important part: What they told me about my birth didn't make me unworthy at all. It's simply how I chose to interpret the story that I heard. I was loved, I mattered. That's what was important. So why did I let it affect me for so many years? Because I didn't realize I had a choice. I was in kindergarten and was pretty literal at that time that mistakes were not something I wanted to be a part of.

What I choose to do with my life and how I interpret the things that are said to me are ultimately up to me. I rewrote my story accurately, maintaining the truth, but with a positive spin. Knowing I was loved from the very beginning makes me wonder why I ever twisted it the first place. I could even call myself a "happy accident," because I know they turn out better than you could have ever planned!

A Great Reason to Write a Book

Thank goodness my mom offered to be one of my magnificent beta readers because she gave me great insight that no one else could have given me. After reading my manuscript, she called me. You know the call, when your mom says she needs to talk to you and straighten you out on a few things? Well I knew I was in trouble even though she didn't even use my middle name—and we needed to do this face to face. Uh oh.

She didn't really think this story was all that important until she read my manuscript. My version of my birth was totally wrong, and maybe I would like to hear the truth? Okay.

I had already known that my dad received the usual government draft letter just before college graduation. He did the draft dodging thing that was popular at the time and immediately got married, mom got pregnant on the honeymoon on cue, and no more fear of the Korean War draft. Or so he thought because he was married with child on the way before the cutoff date.

Fast forward to just after my mom's six-week check-up after my sister was born and my father decided he wanted to have another child right away! Not exactly the time when most women are thinking they would like to get pregnant again. But, no one thought anything of it because it was the 1950s and they both came from Catholic families—in fact, it was almost expected.

A few months after I made my entrance, mom found the second letter that Dad had received but not shared with her: a second draft letter stating that if you didn't have a second child on the way by a certain date, he would be drafted and he did not want to go to war. This changed everything!

I was no mistake! I was his hero! I was the reason he didn't have to go to war, ever. It's like I catapulted from sitting in the corner with the dunce cap on to the head of the class and became the teacher's pet all in one simple sentence!

Two of dad's frat buddies had died early in their Korean War tour, so I understood his fears. My mother's words were, "You were the most planned child possible and the farthest from a mistake you can get," to describe me. Wow, go me.

I actually had a purpose in being born at the exact time and date, as per a government-issued draft letter. That shifts things, but also keeps them the same. I still mattered, I was still loved, now with an additional positive reason though.

It had originally baffled me that the only reason I discovered this true story was because I chose to write a book, but I am eternally grateful for the truth, no matter how I received it. Perception had entered into the story because mom was uncomfortable with it in the first place, so she tucked it away so she wouldn't have to deal with it again. I get it and respect how she chose to deal with it because it was what she thought was best at the time.

The Story of Life Sabotage

I have another whopper of a story that changed my life and I wish it was about something as simple as bike riding, but it's not. To set the stage, it's 1977 and I am an 18-year-old senior in high school discussing college possibilities with my father. This one single story drastically altered my thoughts of who I became for decades. I could entitle it "A sad start to Adulthood" or "College bound for Art School." I also wish that I were making this up, but, unfortunately, I am not.

My Story: All I ever wanted to do when I grew up was go into art. Everyone knew that. My art teacher was very supportive and I had an amazing uncle who was a phenomenal artist. I had the talent, the desire, and was on my way. Nothing was going to stop me! Then one day, a few bombs were dropped on me while talking to my dad about art colleges . . .

Bomb #1 My father told me that he wouldn't support me in any way if I went to art school. He actually forbade me from going into art. How dare he? I had been preparing for this for my whole life; it never occurred to me to have a plan B. Dad told me that if I went to art school, he was sure that I would become an alcoholic like my uncle (artist = automatic alcoholic, I guess?). Sure, I drank several times in high school (drinking age was 18 then), but I was far from an alcoholic.

Bomb #2 Here is the #1 anti-confidence-building tactic to use on your teenage daughter. My dad told me that I was not college material and the only way I would be successful is if I married well (God's truth). I was devastated. In an instant, my existence obviously didn't matter. I was totally in shock.

My mother had never gone to college. My father had bachelor's and master's degrees and had been the personnel manager at a huge, well-known company. So I somehow believed him because of his credentials. I was ranked number 26 in a class of 250, missing the top 10% by one person. (Was I missing something? Why was I not college material? I was a good student with a 3.75 GPA, the first girl to ever take shop classes in wood and metal at my high school, I was active in clubs, worked after school, and created murals and sculptures that the art room still probably has and my counselor and teachers had positive things to say about me—but Dad gave no explanation to counteract these accusations.)

Bomb #3 Unloaded without warning. He then presented me with only three professions that he would support me pursing: Court Reporter, Optometrist Assistant, or Dental Hygienist. (Are you following the Lawyer, Doctor, or Dentist path?) We fought, I cried, and in the end, since I had not saved enough money to run off on my own, ended up in Dental Hygiene school, even though I hated science. I was reassured that I could keep my art on the side if I wanted. Big deal.

Get Your Goddess On!

This changed my respect for my father, the view of myself, and ultimately my whole life in ways that I had never dreamed of, or ever wanted. In a span of an hour, he told me that I wasn't college material, I was not capable of choosing for myself, or able to make it on my own. Great talk, Dad.

My entire being had been altered and there was no turning back after he spewed his story on me as to what he wanted my life to look like. I was dumbfounded, failing to stand up for myself because I was in shock. I had absolutely no self-esteem left to scrape up after the three-bomb conversation. At the time, this was the biggest game changer I had experienced in my entire life. I became a robot child from the shock of it and lived with the fear that if I didn't do what he said, I would be cut off. That's not a great way to live.

Even though I did very well in Dental Hygiene school, my favorite parts of my science-filled college experience were far from science. I excelled in tooth carving, any extracurricular classes, and participating in and winning the snow sculpture contest at the winter carnival for two years in a row. I managed to keep art and creativity into my science-filled college career after all. I discovered that when it's in your blood, it will always be there.

Who was I to question someone as important as my dad who believed his own "made up story" about what my life should look like? So, I unfortunately believed him, too. It just had to be true because he loved me and I trusted him. My mistake was to believe his agenda, his story about me that was filled with his fears and expectations, even though I didn't believe them down deep inside. I allowed his story to become mine even though it wasn't true.

What I came to realize is that they were actually just words made up by my dad. They weren't even about me, they were words, thoughts, and ideas inside of my dad's head. It was his stuff and his fears that he spit out at me—and I chose to believe them. I wasted years.

Not anymore. Remember, you have total control of the stories you tell yourself about you and, even more importantly, what you believe about yourself, from you or anyone else.

By living my dad's version of my life, I became an unhappy storytelling machine who was creating my own little hell. I was stuck in my own pity party, until I finally began to clean off my slate. Do yourself a favor, stop whining and use the rest of this journey to work through whatever stories you've been telling yourself. Think about how to fill in the blank when you say "I'm not enough because_____." When you fill in the blank, start there. This is one of the first steps in getting on your path to know your Goddess. This one event was a giant obstacle in my life for years and kept me from even knowing that an inner power existed.

Three-Step Story Solution

When you are stuck in someone else's story that they are making up about you, here are three simple steps that can help you to decipher what to believe:

> 1. Acknowledge what you know to be true about yourself in their story. Do they have facts to back up their comments? Why are you in their story in the first place? Is anything that they are suggesting to you in your best interest?

> 2. Decide if there is anything in their story that could be helpful to you on your path. Is there a valuable piece that you may not have thought of yet? Could their information send you in a better direction?

3. Throw the rest away and say "Thank you for sharing" to the person. Take only what you need and the rest is just their stuff. You can now hopefully recognize the difference.

Now that you have a plan, please answer these questions honestly. I invite you to have a breakthrough by cleansing out all your old stories to make room for new healthy ones.

Chapter 3 Questions

1. Write the pretend conversation that you want to have with that person who made up a story about you. How do you feel now that you have set the record straight?

_____
_____
_____
_____
_____
_____
_____
_____
_____
_____

The Stories We Tell

2. Tell the story of who told you that you couldn't do something, weren't enough, or didn't matter. How did that affect you? If you could go back, how would you change the story to get a different ending?

_____

_____

_____

_____

_____

_____

_____

_____

3. Make your list of the stories you tell yourself. Positive and negative. Put a T next to the true ones, then change the negative stories to positive by rewriting them with the truth.

_____

_____

_____

_____

_____

Get Your Goddess On!

CHAPTER FOUR

How to Stop Miss Congeniality

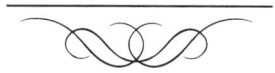

We stop Miss Congeniality with healthy boundaries, that's how. I should know.

Why on earth would anyone want to stop being congenial when they still give awards out for it? Being nice, kind, and thoughtful to others is expected, but when a person takes it to the next level of excessive people pleasing, it becomes unhealthy for them. If you are so focused on pleasing others, it can lead to emotional, mental, and physical issues, where you can lose yourself and end up in a state of dis-ease.

I am officially a *former* congeniality addict. I was so good at it, I didn't even realize I was doing it. Actually, I believe I was raised to be congenial. If you were lucky enough to grow up in one place, you may not know what is required to be the new kid. Conformity was the name of the game, and being congenial was the easiest way to get in with the new crowd. Or at least that's what I thought I was

Get Your Goddess On!

supposed to do. I had no idea that I could stop it with boundaries, because I really didn't know what those were at the time.

As the perpetual new kid, I molded myself into whatever the kids were all about at all seven schools I attended. It was so easy to be made fun of if you didn't fit in with the new group, no wonder I dedicated myself to my excessively congenial craft!

As I grew older, carrying those debilitating ways into my relationships and marriages seemed like a natural progression, since I had congeniality in my blood by then. I was actually happy sometimes and the rest of the time I only pretended to be happy because I knew that's what was expected. Losing sight of what I wanted in life was just one of the many unfortunate byproducts because it felt too risky to dream about personal goals for myself, unless of course, it also benefited others.

After I was married for a few years, I realized that there were other ways to be in a relationship and I began to really rethink my robot wife methods. By socializing with many other couples, I saw glimpses of the kinds of marriages my girlfriends had and became fascinated with observing happy couples. I was enticed by the inclusion of two voices within those relationships.

It was then, in the midst of my mounting personal levels of frustration and being too damn nice, that I started formulating the well-deserved changes to escape from my stifling self-induced crown and banner duties. I discovered that it takes time to crawl out of the deep trench I dug for myself. I guess I didn't realize how long I had been digging.

Then a horrible thought entered the picture: Did I seriously somehow deserve the congenial role I had molded myself into? Easy to think that, because it was all I knew. Did I deserve the more respectful position that I longed for? Oh yes, but I didn't know how.

I fantasized about gaining my own voice in my relationships because I was tired of always being a supporting character in someone else's success story—in my family, on committees, and in my marriage. Watching as they achieved their dreams as I stood by, building them up, while I shriveled inside on the sidelines—how was that working for me? Not so well. I actually felt like a modern-day Cinderella.

My Cinderella Story

Long ago when my daughters and I were taking an online quiz of what Disney princess we identified with, they told me that mine was Cinderella even before I took the quiz! Was it that obvious? It forced me to take a hard look at what example I was setting for them, and I had to face that it really was my story.

Now, after discovering my true self, I can comfortably identify with Cinderella as one of my favorite congenial storybook characters. Think about it: she was able to escape from a very bad situation, rock that five-foot-wide gown, charm the prince, and earn the respect of the kingdom by the time her story was over—all while running around in those beautiful yet uncomfortable glass heels!

In my Cinderella scenario, however, my fairy godmother would be my Goddess and we would do all the work together because she inspires me to own my power! I obviously found the five-foot-wide dress for the cover photo. It amazed me that when I went looking for my idea of a Goddess dress, it ended up looking like Cindy's dress at the ball. If my daughters' observations weren't enough, my choice of Goddess dress was a slam dunk confirmation that I lived, breathed, and somehow wanted to look like her! No sexy, flowing goddess robes and headpiece for me; I identify with the new and powerful Cinderella for my personal vision.

Get Your Goddess On!

I'm happy to say that I also earned my own self-respect because I stood up, looked within, took responsibility, and owned my power. It is a wonderful feeling to be proud of yourself.

I can't be the only woman on this planet to identify with this sweet and innocent heroine. Discovering your Goddess can be like telling your own Cinderella story. It's like magic to watch this young congenial woman transform from one lowly way of being to another more powerful, loving, and confident way. Think of it as Goddess magic.

There was a time in my life that I didn't think I deserved the prince, the ball, the gown, and the castle package. I do now. I believe in the probability of a real happy ending, but since I'm older and wiser now, so I'd also add a few twists to my story.

1. Royal connections would only be optional.

2. We'd exchange actual phone numbers and not deal with my shoe size.

3. Speaking of shoes, I'd go Easy Spirit patent leather low heels—no glass involved.

4. We'd probably have a mortgage, for sure gray hair and some wrinkles.

5. Perhaps both work for a living and on the cusp of retirement thoughts.

6. My waist "might" not be 18 inches like in the movies.

7. This definitely wouldn't happen in one night!

I also want to co-write the script this time because the best way to work on a partnership is together. Maybe we could call the final sequel, "Cinderella & _____ (her Prince) Retire and Travel the World." Of course, we would have to do more research in the form of travel to finalize the script, but I am willing to take one for the team!

Being a Servant or In Service

There is a big difference between being an unappreciated servant (as I had felt I was for years) and being in service to others in a productive and worthwhile way. As a writer, I am most certainly in service to my readers in the most authentically genuine way. To create awareness for you is my daily intention in my writing, coaching calls, and speaking. Even though being a servant and being in service are two totally different things, they are both simply a state of mind to choose.

With the position of servant, it involves being excessively congenial and gives the connotation of being less than others around you. This can be entirely limiting and may possibly stunt any self-worth you potentially have. Lacking control of your life is also most assuredly a part of this unhealthy way of being.

On the other hand, when you are in service, you are fulfilling your purpose here on earth to be in service to others and make your own personal difference in the world. By being in the driver's seat, you can easily control the direction your life goes. Being in service can also look like being on a team like a fundraiser, where everyone works together for a common goal, which is a much healthier place to be in.

Get Your Goddess On!

The Popular Doormat Syndrome, Family Style

Another place in my childhood where congeniality was totally ingrained in my psyche was in the examples of the women and relationships I saw growing up. I witnessed my mother and grandmothers being subservient to the men in their lives, lacking any backbone or voice unless the men were not around. They dutifully stayed home raising children, being obedient, and living with frustrated unhappiness while they were in the position of wife and doormat. They knew their place well.

The only time I saw these women speak with their own voice was when they were doing something they loved, like being a Girl Scout leader, sewing clothes, crocheting throws, playing the piano, or volunteering at school. I saw these areas of life in or outside the house where they greatly excelled and made a difference. Their men supported them in doing these things from a distance, as long as it didn't infringe on the duties of being a wife, mother, and doormat at home.

I nicknamed this scenario the "doormat syndrome" before it was a "thing" in the self-help books. After I had been in my first marriage for just a few months, I saw the tell-tale signs of what I had seen growing up and now that I was in it, I didn't like it. Being a good daughter, I called my mom for advice. She said that I "had made a commitment and should just understand my place, make the best of it, and find some other interests to keep me happy." Seriously.

Several years later, my father died and she felt the taste of freedom. Having taken off her 60+-year-old doormat outfit, she miraculously gave me far different advice. Free of the syndrome, I almost didn't recognize my own mother because she was finally her own person. For the first time in her life, she spoke boldly with a backbone and I almost dropped the phone when she told me that

How to Stop Miss Congeniality

"life is too short to tolerate a man treating you anything less than wonderfully."

This was the beginning of the end of the vicious cycle that had been all I knew. Her transformation was inspirational and was the kick in the butt I needed! I am grateful that my own mother was the first woman to actually show me the drastic transformation from doormat to Goddess by going from 0 to 60 in three seconds! It was actually the first time I saw her love herself fully and I will forever remember her newfound spunk and confidence as she found her power, her Goddess. Thank you, Mom, for your example which also gave me permission to begin the search for my power as well!

Realizing that I actually had a choice, I exercised my new independent muscles, which eventually included getting divorced. Even though many other possible answers were exhausted, in the end, none worked out and we parted ways.

Unfortunately, since I had 37+ years devoted to my old ways and I hadn't yet developed a plan to keep my voice intact, it didn't last and I slipped back to being a semi-doormat in my second marriage, too. I had not realized how far back I had fallen until one night my behavior came into question when my daughters asked me why I always let Daddy win. They also observed that it seemed like it made me sad when I did that. Out of the mouths of babes.

That was my moment of truth. I knew I had to stop showing them that to be a wife and mother meant being a super subservient and congenial doormat. Upon reflection of my own childhood examples, I knew that their lives and the success of their future relationships depended on me to set a healthier example, so I quit cold turkey.

As I found my true voice, it wasn't pretty when the result sadly again was a second divorce. This time I actually stepped into my voice and realized that if I kept doing what I always did, then I would

49

continue to get what I was getting. No more—for the sake of my happiness and my daughters' futures.

I'm proud to say that this doormat syndrome is officially a thing of the past for me. It's been years since I stopped that cycle in honor of my girls. I've done my best to help them feel empowered and enlightened enough to make amazingly better choices than I made long ago. Through our discussions, my example, and society's acceptance of independent women, they have a far better chance of steering clear of this age old and unhealthy syndrome.

Note: Unfortunately, my mom's Goddess transformation had a huge price. My dad was gone. Even though he was definitely not up for any "father of the year" awards, I still loved him. He had a real soft side to him that I got to see sometimes during my life. Believe it or not, I even felt like a daddy's girl sometimes, too. Somehow in the midst of all the muck, I still found things about him to love. He was my dad and I loved him and still miss him today. oxox

The Bag Metaphor

I found an amazing metaphor for my life years later that confirmed why finding my voice was a good thing and it demonstrated how far I'd come. I once had a landscape business with many clients in a very lovely and upscale area of a nearby city. I always felt safe there. It was a Friday afternoon and I was just about to leave when I realized I had forgotten to drop off an invoice for a client. I had left my car for only about three minute when I walked back to see a short, unkempt homeless man with a packed wheelchair standing next to the passenger side of my car with the door now open.

He looked guilty as hell as he took off running, pushing his wheelchair over several of my client files on the ground next to and under my car. As he ran past me, there, under some of his treasures,

How to Stop Miss Congeniality

I saw the handle of my beautiful fabric briefcase sticking out. "OH NO, YOU ARE NOT STEALING MY BAG!" is basically what I screamed at him at full force. I went from sweet, blonde, curly haired, flower Goddess to immediate protective mama bear in the blink of an eye! I was the Goddess of Fury and there was nothing getting between me and my precious bag!

That bag contained current client files yet to be invoiced, my wallet with all my credit cards, $30 cash, and the checkbook that actually had money in it. This was not going to happen. I chased him; I grabbed it as he shouted harassing remarks at me, while I looked through the contents and he sped away. I wondered, where the heck did that courage come from?

I stopped running and dialed the police, then it dawned on me what had actually just happened. I was furious but not at all fearful. Not at all. That surprised me, feeling amazingly proud and foolish at the same time. Proud because I had just stood up for myself in the most powerful way ever and foolish because he could have had a weapon and I had no fear. Oops!

I cried as I drove home because I had just experienced a beautiful metaphor for my life. For most it, I just sat there as people stole things from me while I was being too congenial. I didn't know how to stop them, or even if I could, and still be liked.

I had basically given other people permission to take my voice, my dignity, my self-worth, and self-esteem. Could I have prevented my power from being stolen out from under me if I had just found my voice, my power, my courage earlier? Yes. Where would I be now and how would my life be different if I had discovered I could do this for myself long ago? Thoughts and speculations flooded in and I was in shock from the what ifs.

Get Your Goddess On!

In one instant, I had transformed into the powerfully proactive person I had always wanted to be. Somewhere on my path with my Goddess, I figured out that it was okay to take action, instead of backing down to allow people to take my things me, as I watched. I felt empowered enough to be able to do what I feared I couldn't do—both keep my stuff and not care at all if the guy stealing from me liked me at all! After that event, I liked and respected myself more than I ever had before. I was finally proud of who I had become. About time!

The truth is I always had the choice to do something, but didn't feel powerful or smart enough to do anything about it. I felt transformed and vindicated because I decided that I finally mattered and I could protect myself. What a beautiful lesson he taught me, I thought, as I drove home and smiled as I cried. Thank you, old man.

There are no accidents. The serendipitous part of the story is that about an hour before this all happened, I received a phone call from the local rescue mission that feeds the homeless at the shelters in the city I was in. They were looking for pledges for a donation matching campaign and I made a $25 phone pledge.

When the donation card came in the mail a few days later, I made a check out for $50 and wrote a note on the card saying that I was doubling my donation because I wanted to make sure that the little old man that walks around the city pushing a wheelchair gets extra meals and extra care so he doesn't have to steal from people. I kissed the back of the envelope before I mailed it. Love and blessings, old man.

Do You Have It?

Let's have some fun now and take a 10-question quiz to see if you have the Miss Congeniality Syndrome. Please answer honestly to get a real indication of where you are.

Answer yes or no to the following 10 questions and keep track of your yes answers.

The Miss Congeniality Quiz

1. Do you regularly say yes when you want to say no (and vice versa)?

2. Have you lost your "voice" at home, work, in your relationship, or all three?

3. Do you frequently check with someone before you answer (or do you have to be careful how you answer)?

4. Do you walk on eggshells with anyone?

5. Are you regularly without an opinion of your own because you're afraid to say it?

6. Do you change your view of something based on who you are with?

7. Are there people that you avoid being with because you feel inferior when you are with them?

8. Do you care more about how others think about you than your own thoughts and opinions about yourself?

Get Your Goddess On!

9. Have you changed your hair, way you dress, what you do, or how you are in life based on someone else's opinion of you?

10. Do you alter what you want out of life, based on what relationship you are in at the time?

Scoring

8–10 Yes Answers
You need intervention to find out who you are again. You wear the Congeniality Syndrome t-shirt everywhere you go. Please practice saying no and voicing your opinion in the bathroom mirror! If you have truly forgotten what your opinion is, have lunch with a friend that scored in the 1–3 or 0 categories and she will give you the pep talk you desperately need!

4–7 Yes Answers
You are on your way to losing yourself, but you can still snap out of it and take that t-shirt off. Practice your "no" responses and what you are going to say when you feel yourself falling back into the endless state of congeniality. Repeat daily as needed.

1–3 Yes Answers
You still know who you are and haven't put the t-shirt on yet. Congrats, you are conscious of the state of excessive congeniality, but know you are strong enough to avoid it most of the time now that you are aware of a better life. Please help your friends who are in the categories with more yeses!

0 Yes Answers
Congratulations! Your Goddess is on and you are your own woman! Make a reservation for lunch now to help out your 8-10 yes friends and be gentle and ruthless at the same time!

I'm not proud of it, but for decades while I was at the height of my congeniality, I was a 10 yes kind of girl—and that's not something to brag about either. If I could go back in a time machine, being so dang congenial would be one of the first things I would change. That and my 11th-grade unfortunate haircut and perm.

The quiz is fun but serious because every one of these things unfortunately continues to happen every day as women still give their power away. For some, it's all they know and others know it's wrong, but they don't know how to get out. For all of us former addicts, we know there is a way out.

I never liked being so congenial, and I felt disappointed in myself and angry that I had let myself be taken advantage for so long. I imagine that I'm not the only one who has been angry at myself for wearing that dang banner for way too long. I regularly took my frustrations out on myself with loads of self-punishment and "less than" type of self-talk. This is what perpetuates the horrible cycle of the momentum of abuse alive and well in so many areas of our lives. Remember, a girl can only be so nice for so long if she is pretending so much.

I actually know of a beautiful real life Miss Congeniality who ended up in the hospital for many months with stress-related conditions that kept her almost paralyzed. It's a real thing.

Now What?

If you are ready to end this by taking your banner off, then start with the following steps to help yourself get out and stay out of the Miss Congeniality Syndrome. They worked for me. Repeat as needed.

1. **Trust and love yourself** where you are right now, regardless of where that is.

2. Research your personal history to see how you got so deep into congeniality. Look for the steps you took and **forgive yourself** for each of those steps along the way as you officially climb out of your trench. Be grateful for every step on the way out.

3. Please **choose a new belief in yourself**, make new choices and attitudes. Write ideas down and define yourself as to what you want to look like. Choose the "tone" of your new voice.

4. **Treat yourself differently**, now with respect! Repeat regularly, "I matter!"

5. **Train the people in your life to treat you differently**, now with respect. Sit down with people in your life, if necessary, and communicate with sincerity and compassion. Read them this chapter if you need some reinforcement. Show them you matter by your behavior and new way of being. Boundaries with other people are crucial!

6. **Write your fears on slips of paper** and put them in a paper bag, crumple it up, and drop it on the floor in the back seat of your car so you will never find them again. They will still be with you, but in a very unimportant way. Clean out car as needed.

7. **Baby steps or giant leap**—take your pick, see what works for you and move forward.

8. **Ask for help if you need it.** Smart people know when they need help. Sister Goddesses are great for supportive, authentic points of view and can be amazing sounding boards!

9. Remember that there is nothing authentic about being excessively congenial. Time to **take your power back and put a game plan together**. Use these guidelines to begin.

10. **Create a healthy compromise plan** where you can still be nice, yet keep your own voice and power. The solution serves both people involved in the situation and the effort goes both ways. The end result is that you still believe in yourself enough to follow your dreams with confidence, at the same time you care and respect for yourself and others. These are the beginnings of your new healthy boundaries and maintenance program.

Congenial Movies

I obviously didn't invent the concept of excessive congeniality. Over the years, there have been many characters in films that I saw myself in. Five of my favorite movies with leading overly congenial female characters that I can relate to are modern classics in their own right: 27 Dresses, Runaway Bride, The Holiday, The Wedding Date, and, of course, Miss Congeniality. Watch them in the name of research and see if you recognize yourself in the characters. Popcorn optional.

How to Stop Congeniality
with New Healthy Boundaries

Are you done being overly congenial yet? It's exhausting. After years of giving too much of yourself away, isn't it finally time to keep some of you for you? The perfect fix for being a terminal people pleaser is healthy boundaries. Boundaries come in two categories: 1) healthy and 2) negatively limiting.

Healthy boundaries are a necessary part of maintaining positive self-respect and high levels of self-worth, because they are based on respect and created by us, for us. They are helpful parameters we identify with to keep us safe, have fun, but still feel in control. They are also usually the farthest point you can go yet still comfortable. Often just knowing that they are there will give us the permission to say no and actually stop us from crossing a line, so we maintain our quality of life.

Do you remember back when someone else set up boundaries for you as a young child, when you couldn't go past the end of the driveway? What about in high school when you had a curfew to be home with dad's car by 11 pm? I like to think of healthy boundaries as a safety net, knowing I can still live fully, yet I've got my own back, so to speak. That's because I'm conscious of the limits of what I think is acceptable and can still feel safe and proud of myself.

My self-pronounced boundaries have gotten broader as I got older, then again smaller as I've aged. I believe it has to do with fears and the amount of freedom I'm comfortable with. I had far fewer fears and gave myself much more freedom in my teens and 20s. I started having babies in my 30s, so I began to narrow up those old freer boundaries. Now in my 50s, I'm a bit more comfortable with them reined in to keep me protected because my perception of fears and freedoms have changed over the years.

Most of us have personal boundaries already set up for things like financial investing, drinking and driving, and dating/relationships. Each of these areas could produce profoundly negative consequences if we fail to pay attention to them. By monitoring and assessing our situations regularly, it's easy to maintain the higher quality of life we strive for.

Altering Our Awareness

Drugs and alcohol are two things that can very easily alter our healthy boundaries without fully realizing their effects until later. Today, I don't drink by choice even though I'm around it regularly. I didn't always abstain, but many years ago I simply made a choice to stop. Since your healthy boundaries are made for you, by you, you can simply give yourself permission to change your boundaries to match where you are in life.

Once, I had a friend throw her personal boundaries away because of the influences of a bad boyfriend, then she got involved in drugs and alcohol. The results she achieved by chucking her boundaries produced far more frustrations and problems—along with a much lower quality of life. She started to believe that she deserved the bad things that were happening to her because she was worthless and didn't feel that she mattered. Unfortunate and hard to watch, but it was her choice in the end. I could talk, coach, and listen to her, but I couldn't re-create her boundaries for her; she had to do it for herself. Eventually she did and is now counseling other women because of the lessons she learned.

It's important to realize if your boundaries are regularly being compromised by drugs or alcohol. Please pay attention if this applies to you because help is always available. Treatment can improve your quality of life if you really want the help, because you are worth it.

Friendly Fences Are Healthy Boundaries

Sometimes we put respectful boundaries in place for protection from people, things, and outside negative influences that are around us. Let's think of them as friendly fences that correlate with the needs in our lives.

Fences are boundaries we can touch. Some say fences make good neighbors. I think there is some truth to that. Have you ever had a next door neighbor with a dog that prefers to poop in your yard, as opposed to their own? Or neighborhood kids who regularly run around in your flower beds playing tag, chasing balls, or picking your flowers?

Fences also help greatly with the question of property lines from a legal point of view. My personal favorite reasons for fences are for privacy, around swimming pools, and vegetable gardens. The purpose of a fence is to keep things and people out and keep people and things in. Now let's talk about them in real life.

The healthy boundaries that we make for ourselves are like invisible fences to help create a happier life. Some people want to dump on us, make us chase after unreasonable demands, and take things from us like time and respect—but only if we let them. If you allow people to disrespect you in any way, or you have an addiction to always being liked, it costs you more than you realize. No more—that's where healthy boundaries are helpful.

By creating these, you honor yourself by establishing how you want to be treated. They can also be fun, easy, and make life more abundantly happy by setting the parameters of where we feel safe, yet still live well.

The purpose of our boundaries is to keep things and people out that are not respecting us and sometimes taking advantage of us.

How to Stop Miss Congeniality

They allow us to keep our self-respect, worth, and safety intact. If we feel safe, respected, and realize our personal value and self-worth, life can be more enjoyable and we feel more in control of our lives.

The golden key is that they are usually put in place for a reason or to solve a problem. Some boundaries are established to protect us, some guard us, and some save lives every day, all day. An example of these are guard rails, white and yellow lines, and shoulders on the sides of our roads everywhere. These guidelines and extra protection are part of a valuable preventive boundaries system to save our lives physically. Your personal healthy boundaries you set up for yourself are usually for physical and/or emotional reasons or benefits.

Workplace Boundaries

Workplace boundaries are crucial for the Miss Congenialities of the office and can help provide a healthy work environment. Maintaining your values, communication, and knowing the rules are your best allies when in a potentially compromising situation at work. The workplace boundaries are usually established in the form of a policy, then put in place to protect and respect all employees.

As a dental hygienist, I only once felt physically threatened and once felt strong sexual advances from two different dentists who gave me the creeps. Neither were fun experiences and since there were no official policies set up at either of the tiny offices, it was the boss's word against mine. The odds were not in my favor if I wanted to keep my job.

In those situations, I was limited as to what I could do, so I found other employment immediately. Since I knew what my boundaries were when these events came up, it was an easy choice to support myself to only work at places where they valued and respected me as an employee. Standing my ground reinforced my self-respect, and I felt comforted to know how much importance I had put on my own personal value and safety.

I was lucky to be clear and confident in handling these work situations. Unfortunately, I know of women who feel intimidated and concerned about their position if they turn down unwanted gestures by bosses or coworkers. To them, by ignoring those advances, it could jeopardize their future at the company. It's almost as if they think that their job and congenially climbing the corporate ladder are more important than self-respect. Nothing is more important than you. Start treating yourself that way.

Another subtle physical boundary that can also be seen is our body language. The most obvious one that comes to mind from a meeting I attended was the arm crossing gesture that signified the person was not open to what I was saying. When he crossed his arms, it immediately presented a challenge and appeared that he was totally closed to my ideas. It told me "no" before my presentation ever began.

To diffuse his negative boundary, I looked for a way to hand him a few pieces of paper so he had to unfold his arms to receive the information I was giving him. Watch your own body language and see if your communication at work improves.

On the job, be both respected and safely protected. Get help immediately if you feel threatened in any way. You'd be surprised how damaging an experience like this can be if not diffused quickly. Please report inappropriate behavior to the proper channels at work. You and your personal value are at stake. No one ever needs to tolerate being treated disrespectfully to get ahead in *any situation*, period!

Teaching People How to Treat Me 101

This is my job because I am in charge of me. I have been treated horribly because for a very long time, I taught them how to do it and didn't know any better. Now I do. Here are my top five ideas to begin your personal **Teach People How to Treat Me 101** course:

1. **Respect yourself.** If you don't respect you, neither will they. You must also earn the respect of others by being respectful. Give it, if you expect to receive it. The best way to teach people how to respect you is by your actions and life example.

2. **Be worthy of all the goodness around you.** Do you establish your worthiness based on how much you do for others? Do you value it based on what you contribute to your family? Job? Church? Relationships? Do you regularly identify your own worthiness as to what you give away instead of what you feel you are worthy of receiving? I did.

   Worthiness is not about excessive giving at all. It's about how open you are to receiving all the goodness of life from this wonderfully abundant universe. To help you grasp this concept of worthiness, I found an amazing quiz that only takes a few minutes to complete. The results will show you where you stand on the worthiness scale in several areas of your life. This information can help you create a more enjoyable and receptive quality of life.

   Terri Britt is a nationally known author and speaker who has created this insightful online quiz called The Worthiness Quotient. It is a fun and helpful way for you to see how open or closed you are to receiving the greatness you desire in your life. She assists you in the most respectful ways, to be more open and deserving to receive. She's an authentic Goddess who lives in a place of love, passion, abundance, and prosperity every day. Go to www.theworthinessquotientquiz.com immediately to take the quiz.

I was intrigued by my results and really fascinated by my numbers in a couple areas. It allowed me to rethink how I am receiving. For too long in my life I was on automatic for giving and not as open to receiving. This quiz made me stop and wonder if I was forgetting to receive, or thinking I didn't deserve to receive. Very interesting. In the Supportive Resources chapter, there is more information on other books and downloads available from Terri and how to contact this amazing woman.

3. **Matter.** Participate in life 100% and own your Goddess and who you are. Be the example that you want to be. Know that you play a role in this world that is important because it wouldn't be the same without you. Treat yourself like you matter every day.

4. If you don't already have **healthy boundaries** in place, look at your past experiences to see where you felt you let your guard down. Also, look for times when someone disrespected you or you were unhappy with how you were treated. Think of the times you wanted a life do-over, because of a result that you weren't happy with or you

didn't handle something well. Did you go too far, not far enough? Think about the outcome you would want for yourself, or how you could handle things differently. These are places you need to establish your comfort levels and are the places to strengthen boundaries.

This is a process that continues to evolve, so start here and own these new boundaries to help you feel more in control of your life. When we feel safe, cared for, and respected, we are more accountable and genuine in every aspect of our lives.

5. **Follow through and be authentic with your boundaries and trust yourself.** If you are trustworthy, honest, and thoughtful, you will attract the same type of people to you and they will treat you similarly. This is another example of the Law of Attraction: what you put out to the world comes back to you because it's reflecting who you are in the world. Follow through is crucial to also earn what you desire.

The Success Rate

Does this always work? No. When you teach people in your life how to treat you in a new way, it is possible that not everyone will be a star pupil. Some people may still continue to disrespect you, make snide remarks, or expect you to continue to cave under their unrealistic demands, like you did before when you were overly congenial. After all, you did train them quite well.

Those persistently negative people may not make the cut in the end. I experienced this exact scenario when I was in my own re-teaching phase. I actually let those people go and rejoiced to feel that sweet release of the old, unwelcomed disrespect they continued to give me. My life got tremendously better in so many ways because I no longer allowed myself to be pulled down by their attitudes, actions, and negative treatment—and I didn't miss them at all.

Have you ever noticed that when you tolerate bad behavior from kids or dogs, it only gets worse? Adults are just big kids in older clothes. I've had my fill of bullies in my life and had unfortunately gotten too comfortable with that type of behavior. I'm not proud to say I was numb to it and still felt I somehow deserved it in my life. It took me many years and compassionate effort to finally set up safe and healthy boundaries for myself. Just because I was once tolerant doesn't mean I had to stay that way.

Experience and knowledge did wonders to alter my tolerance level for disrespectful abuse. A couple of years ago, I met a man who seemed wonderful at first. During our first conversation, he was on his best behavior and quite charming. On our first official date, he was mildly disrespectful to our waitress and he thought it was funny. He didn't get a second date.

Because you are the person setting your life up, there's no reason you can't alter your tolerance level as needed. I'm happy to report that my once very high tolerance for abuse is down to zero now. Use your healthy boundaries as guidelines setting your tolerance levels and always exercise your right to say "I'm done" when you need to.

Your Goddess knows how to say "no" in the most beautiful ways; trust her and give yourself permission to protect you from all types of bullies and their abuse. Look around your life and see how many different types of abusive people you have attracted into your circle, then re-teach them or let them go.

Negative Boundaries as Limitations

The other type of boundaries that people can develop are negative limitations. These are like good boundaries gone wrong. They can severely cripple any possibility of happiness, love, or enjoyment in life, depending on the severity.

These can be mild and just slightly limiting so that you let fear or the what-ifs run your life. There may or may not be any particular reason for the mild to severe limitations to be there, but they feel like a self-induced ball and chain program that keeps you too safe and prevents you from living fully. With introspection, discovery, new choices, and perspective, you can shift out of these limiting ways of thinking. Ask for help if you are having difficulties.

Then there are other more serious limitations that can be much worse and almost invisible, that we put on ourselves and may not be easy to see. These little nasties can be added in an instant, but take years to remove. They can also be devastating and overpowering to even the best of us, leaving us feeling like we didn't have a choice. Unfortunately, many times this happens after some form of trauma. Even though I personally don't remember giving these horrible limitations permission to engulf me, I must've nodded off because my life was taken over in an instant.

These stifling mental and physical limitations that affected me go by the name of posttraumatic stress disorder, or PTSD. For me to relive being raped over and over, to wake up clutching parts of my body to protect myself again and again . . . while feeling very betrayed and unsafe for years, put a definite damper on my life and kept me from living fully. I lived a life filled with blame, fear, guilt, mistrust, and the feeling that I somehow deserved to be treated that way.

At the time I was living with it, I had no idea that this thing had a name and was very afraid that it would last forever. Fortunately, I was wrong. It went away for me, with many of the continued efforts that I share with you in this book. I didn't actually realize it, until I finished writing the first draft, but my journey of crawling out from under my negative limitations coincided with the discovery of my Goddess. The positive personal power I gained was the best way I learned to combat those limitations.

As I searched for a solution to a problem that was way bigger than me, I knew that finding great help was the key. That's why I kept searching until I found the answers. If you choose to just muddle through it alone, you may be stuck for years feeling the residual effects, like I did. If I would have known that a spectacular person like Jo Standing existed, it would have made my life a lot easier. She is an amazingly giving soul that wrote a holistic healing book called *Conquer Trauma Drama: Get Your Life Back*. There is also a wonderful coordinating workbook to enhance your healing experience even further.

Phenomenally positive things happen when you get the right help and learn how to love yourself again! Jo also heads up The Trauma Drama Coaching Institute, speaking nationally to help people with PTSD, anxiety, and depression with holistic trauma recovery methods. If you recognize that this is a negative limitation for you, please get help now. More information about how to contact Jo is also in the Supportive Resources chapter—you will be very happy you found this ray of sunshine in a sea of gray uncertainty! Her Goddess is on and is very healing!

I'm hoping that you are starting to recognize your Goddess and can feel the intuitive powers within. Healthy boundaries enhance the quality of your life. When you live within the parameters of what you view as a safe, comforting, and healthy, you know you are home! Let's start with honoring yourself and respecting your own boundaries while you teach people how you want to be treated.

Sometimes our greatest successes are actually found in our yuckiest challenges. The wisdom we gain from the adversity we live through is profound. If we all adopted a pay it forward kind of attitude to help those who are still in it, once we are out of it, love and compassion levels would be at an all-time high. I discovered that the valuable knowledge we attain can be of better use when shared. As you cleanse through your stuff, is there someone else you can reach out to to help them cleanse and clarify in some small way?

Chapter 4 Questions

1. Have you ever been too congenial and it's gotten you into trouble, created frustration, or made you feel like you weren't enough? If you were given a life do-over, what would you do differently?

_____

_____

_____

_____

_____

_____

_____

Get Your Goddess On!

_____

_____

_____

2. What was your score for the Miss Congeniality quiz? What is your plan to avoid excessive congeniality in the future?

_____

_____

_____

_____

_____

_____

_____

_____

3. Do the Worthiness Quotient Quiz online at www.theworthinessquotientquiz.com, if you haven't already. Write your numbers down and jot notes about what you can do to raise some of the lower scores.

_____

_____

_____

4. What are the healthy boundaries you have set up for yourself already? Do you need to make changes to them to enhance the quality of your life? Give details.

CHAPTER FIVE

Mistakes and Lessons

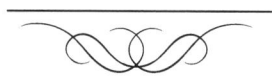

Mistakes have a bad reputation. In this chapter, I hope you learn to embrace your mistakes and be inspired by the knowledge you learn from them to share with others. In fact, I think we learn faster through our mistakes, when we embrace those lessons wholeheartedly.

I know that I have already made more mistakes than I'm probably supposed to have made by now. I seriously hope that no one is actually keeping score, but I'm afraid somewhere, there is a long tally sheet with my name on it that I will have to answer to someday!

As we continue with our party preparations, all the planning and setting up is well underway. What if you go to the grocery store and pick up all the trays for the party and accidentally leave the last cheese tray on the bottom of one of the carts and you don't notice until much later? You made a mistake; will you react with an "oh well" or "oh shit"?

Do you react with intensity or respond with clarity and reason? Do you panic, scream, beat yourself up, or do you look at the other six trays of delicious food and realize that it was the second cheese tray and was to be used as backup anyway? Will the guests feel that they are being slighted? No. Will you continue to feel like a failure because one extra tray is missing, or will you let it go and move on, knowing that your guests are arriving in about an hour and you still need to finished getting dressed? Do you prioritize your time or is every battle yours to fight? Think about how you relate to making a mistake as we journey into mistakes and lessons.

Let's start the conversation that you have always wanted to have, but just didn't know it, by addressing mistakes in no particular order.

The Top 10 Things I Learned about Mistakes

1. **Anyone can make an infinite number of mistakes.** There are unfortunately no limits or age restrictions on this prolific activity. I'm still waiting to outgrow it.

2. **I put mistakes in four main categories: small, medium, large, and gigantic.** The value you place on how serious your mistake is depends on your personal perspective. Please remember that this is not a contest to see who has the worst mistakes.

3. **Happy accidents can happen in any of the four categories.** They can be thought of as a mistake at first, then turn into something wonderfully positive in the end. Usually there is a time lapse associated with this type of mistake, and it can end up to being a fabulous experience.

Mistakes and Lessons

An example of this is when a roofer tarped my house poorly. A storm came up and in 25 minutes, I had $30,000 damage to my new little fixer upper—before I even made my first mortgage payment! Half of the things that ended up getting redone because of the damage (and paid for by insurance) were projects I hadn't planned on for phase one of remodeling. The whole experience was a big hassle, inconvenient, and took forever.

Only half of the house was livable for six months and I was at the end of my rope until . . . I realized how much of my house had been fixed and how wonderful it all looked afterward. I was way ahead of my three-year remodeling plan, too. Happy accidents usually end up amazingly positive!

Another example of a heartwarming happy accident with a sweet ending involved a young woman, a surprise pregnancy, and a one-night stand in college. She cried for a week, was very hard on herself, and wondered if her happy life was over. But, she ended up loving motherhood and raised her daughter to be a happy, healthy, and very sweet little girl.

A few years later, the young woman got married and wanted to have more children with her new husband. They had difficulties and found out that she had major fibroid tumors and wasn't able to have any more children. This sweet little girl who was once thought of as a mistake ended up being her cherished miracle child! Her new daddy adopted and adored her and the woman finally understood that things happen for sometimes unexpected reasons. Happy accidents are usually fully understood only later on and can be blessings disguised as people.

4. **Mistakes are really just life lessons in disguise.** If we don't choose to treat our mistakes as lessons, then we are destined to repeat those same mistakes over and over again in bigger ways until we learn the intended lesson.

In my opinion, this is the most important one on the list. Mistakes are definitely most powerful when used as a learning tool. When we learn from our mistakes, it creates a new part of us that is hopefully smarter. That lesson learned also becomes part of who we are and adds to our knowledge to help us make choices in our future.

Here's the good news: We re-create ourselves with every step of our journey, mistakes included. So, mistakes are not so bad after all—but they sure can derail us, even on a good hair day. The bad news is that if we don't learn from our lessons, we really are destined to relive our mistakes often in bigger and more obvious ways . . . again and again, until we learn the intended lesson

This is the part of the big game of life where I racked up tally points like a pinball machine on that fateful list. I thought those things were just happening to me (victim mentality) and, for many years, had no idea that there was a lesson in there—that's probably why I kept repeating myself. (Did I say that already?) I think of mistakes and their subsequent lessons in a totally different way now, like a free gift with purchase!

5. **We beat ourselves up about our mistakes.** Usually this includes blame, shame, guilt, frustration, victim mentality, and sometimes self-destructive behavior.

   This puzzles me. Why do we beat ourselves up about making mistakes? It was just a mistake, something we did that didn't work out. Why can't we appreciate it as the lesson it was, fix it, and move on? I think this is why self-punishment has become rampant and we simply don't need to do it. It is also one of the biggest sources of giving our power away and feeds our negative self-talk, which is just a waste of time and robs us of even more power.

   We bury our Goddesses by regularly practicing self-punishment. It's time to choose to stop beating yourself up by objectively looking at your mistakes as lessons and forgive yourself in the process. Let's become students of problem solving instead.

6. **Even as an authentic Goddess, we still make mistakes,** but they end up looking more like conscious choices gone bad that you learn a lesson from. Usually they are easier and more efficient to process and include immediate acknowledgment, accountability, and responsibility. In other words, they are handled on a higher level.

Why does our inner Goddess still allow us to make mistakes? Because these mistakes/lessons are part of our pathway of life to show us the way. Most of us have piled all the blame, shame, guilt, frustration, victim mentality, and self-destructive behavior on top of our Goddess. It makes sense that we will have a few layers to uncover on our path to find our power.

Our lessons that we learn from the mistakes we make will help to access the power within when we deal with them successfully and peel off the layers. The more awareness that we have when we reveal the truth about what we've been doing to ourselves, the easier it is to unlock the path to our power. Sometimes we can't quite put our finger on "her" unless we search. This book is the search.

It also helps to get away from our mistakes/problems in order to see them. If you stay on the ground, you will never see the vastness of our earth. If we don't climb some hills or mountains along the way, we can't appreciate the view of all we can see when we reach the top. Look at yourself as a whole from a distance first, in order to see the details of the magnificent you and your Goddess. You need to see that you are more than your mistakes.

7. **No matter what we do to help our kids to prevent repeating our mistakes, they will still repeat some of ours and make many new and improved mistakes of their own. Period.**

8. **We are all human and will continue to make mistakes because none of us are perfect** 100% of the time. Parents are not perfect and can sometimes make mistakes for the whole family. Politicians are also not perfect and can make mistakes for a nation.

9. **I don't like making mistakes or being on the receiving end of mistakes.** When I do make them, I feel an apology is a must for what was done and to whom it was done to.

   This is a very important and often forgotten point. "Woman up" ladies: when you make a mistake, apologize to the person involved, even if that someone is you. Being humble and admitting any wrong doing by taking responsibility is the first place to start with any mistake you make. Without it, the mistake just stays there and festers.

   This sometimes gets tricky when you feel you are apologizing for something you did and the other person sees it totally differently. Stay with what you honestly know you did. Perception added into any situation can complicate everything. Stick to the facts.

10. **The New and Improved Mistake Formula**

    Choice + Questionable Result = Mistake (sometimes)

    Mistake + Recalculation done immediately based on Results + Accountability = Lesson

I have already admitted that I have made plenty of whopping mistakes. I regularly asked myself "What was I thinking?" and "How is that working for you?" Now, when I feel I've made a mistake, I learn from it immediately by looking at my results.

The shift is much more positive if you are living with accountability as one of your partners—that's the key that has made all the difference for me. By changing how I think about mistakes, I feel smarter because it's easier to learn from my experiences. A bonus is that I have stopped beating myself up with this simple shift and have gotten amazing results.

When you make a choice and get a less than desired result, then you might call it a mistake. Take that mistake and recalculate it based on what happened (the result); add in your own accountability as to what part you played in the event and what you could do to change the outcome. Then make that difference to change the result and discover your lesson.

Your own accountability is the key to personally owning your mistake. What you learn from it becomes knowledge and that knowledge is used in future choices hopefully, so that your lesson learned prevents future repetition of the same event. Trust me, being a late bloomer on this was not a good thing.

Let's use mathematics as an example here. If you continue to do algebra, geometry, or calculus using the wrong formulas or incorrect specific mathematical equations, you will continue to get the same wrong answers. What you consistently put into something, you will consistently get the same thing out. Numbers and formulas don't usually lie, unless of course you put the wrong information in.

I'm never proud of making a mistake, but it is empowering to face them, learn from them, and rise above.

Yesterday's Breakfast

To give your mistakes more attention is to give them power; I choose to keep my power.

If you spent time and effort on the mistakes you made yesterday, you would be wasting time today and preventing yourself from enjoying the present. Who really needs to worry about something that is already gone?

Things that had once affected our lives can be reduced to just something that happened in the past once you have dealt with it. Since they don't matter anymore, I like to refer to them as "yesterday's breakfast."

Does it really matter what you ate for breakfast yesterday? No. As long as it gave sustenance to your physical machine called a body to get you through your day, who cares? No one. Granola with plump blackberries and honey vanilla yogurt, who cares? Spinach quiche with mushrooms and Swiss cheese . . . donuts . . . cold pizza . . . all delicious, but done, gone, finished. Who cares? None of them matter after they've been eaten.

Get Your Goddess On!

The same can be said for mistakes and old relationships. You have moved on, so they are also yesterday's breakfast. When you focus on the rear view mirror while driving, I guarantee that it will cause problems as you are hurling your vehicle forward on the highway of life. It truly is a waste of time and effort to focus on the past. You can't do anything about the past and the future is yet to be determined, so be present.

Remember my example of my dad and our college conversation? I now treat it with the same importance as a half grapefruit, guava nectar, and a piece of bacon, which was my breakfast recently. It frankly doesn't deserve any more attention than that. Why would I want to give my power to something that happened 40 years ago, seriously? It's gone and I learned the lesson I needed to. Move on and keep your power at the same time!

For a visual, let's imagine that you ate your breakfast in the car this morning on your way to work. If the oatmeal bowl is not removed when you get home, it will still be sitting in your back seat the next morning. It will literally be yesterday's breakfast bowl in your back seat. What if it stays there for a week? It would get pretty disgusting even after a couple days, let alone 40 years of sitting in the back seat. Gross.

What a ridiculous thing to do, isn't it? Many of us do it regularly; I know I did. Let's keep yesterday's breakfast where it belongs: once appreciated, but now gone. Cleaning out the bowls from your backseat is what we are doing by the way.

Did I always feel this way? No. I gave away lots of my power to silly events for so many years. Can you imagine giving away 75% of your life? I did. The reason I kept giving my power away to someone else is because I didn't realize that I had the choice to keep it. Now we all know. Time to own your mistakes and the lessons that come with them, but let them go after dealing with them because they don't deserve your power, attention, or to matter anymore.

Chapter 5 Questions

1. List five positive things you identify with about making mistakes.

___

___

___

___

___

___

___

___

___

___

2. What are your top mistakes you've made and the subsequent lessons you learned from them?

___

___

___

___

___

Get Your Goddess On!

_____
_____
_____
_____
_____

3. Which of your mistakes still have your power and what do you need to do to shift them into yesterday's breakfast?

_____
_____
_____
_____
_____
_____
_____
_____
_____
_____
_____
_____
_____

CHAPTER SIX

The Avoidance Zone

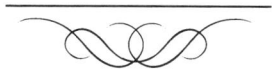

You can't avoid things forever. Sooner or later, they will catch up with you.

Your party is just about to begin and you are almost ready. There are last-minute things to tuck away, so that people only see the party you, not how you really live. Because you are still cleansing, you want people to see only what you want them to see and to remember your party as an event of the season. Heaven forbid they see the real you yet.

I wish that we all liked everything about ourselves. The world would be happier, but we don't, so let's start dealing with one thing at a time. First thing to do is own up to the fact that you have this stuff you don't want anyone to see stashed all over the place. Pretending that you don't only makes it worse.

Once, I dated a guy for a while who would actually coach me on the way to the party, about what to say and what not to say to the people at the party, so that he would look better. Because I was in full on people-pleasing mode at the time, I did as I was told and beefed up my guy to appear better than he was. I now realize that I was in the "shallow zone" of dating and it got me to wonder why people have to hide things in order to get ahead. Of course, I wasn't hiding anything, but other people were . . .

The truth is that I discovered that I couldn't escape from the prison I put myself in with all my self-punishment, subservience, and victim mindset because I didn't actually know I was in there until I felt really stuck. So, I asked myself, why do we avoid the obvious things about ourselves that could actually guide us to the freedom that we long for? There are so many healthy directions to go in, right in front of us, but for some reason, so often, many of us choose to wallow.

Entering Your Avoidance Zone

Now that we've explored mistakes, it's time to address all the other things we don't want to think about, talk about, or write about. We go to all costs to avoid these things that also unknowingly negatively affect the way we live our lives. It's time to go below the surface and enter . . . the avoidance zone. This is where all the stuff we have pushed away goes, so no one can see the real person we are, not even us.

When I'm staging a house to go on the market, I run into people who don't really want to clean out their garage, attic, basement, or closets. It's like pulling teeth to get their cooperation sometimes because that's where they store all the things they don't want to deal with until they absolutely have to. Funny thing is, if you leave it all there, it doesn't magically go away by itself. Go figure.

If they did something about all the stuff *now*, the house would look amazing when buyers walk around, feeling welcomed instead of

The Avoidance Zone

overwhelmed. How often do people try to camouflage their excess stuff while pretending that no one sees the piles and piles of it in every corner'?

We do the exact same thing to our inner selves. We may look really good on the outside, like everything is perfect, but on the inside, you may be stuffed with everything but perfection when you begin to explore within.

All this extra stuff we don't know what to do with, or how to get rid of, or if we are ready to part with yet just stays there in our avoidance zone until we figure it out or we totally go on overload by breaking down or blowing up.

To get a visual, imagine moving your parents out of their home after living there for 40 years. The accumulation can be massive and the job is probably way too much for one person to handle alone. This is what we do to ourselves. No wonder we feel so heavy, so burdened, and continue to feel overwhelmed with life and underwhelmed with ourselves. We have 40 years of "stuff" to deal with all at once.

Avoiding things comes naturally to most, as if it were in our genes. I admit that I saved many a thing in my zone that I didn't want to deal with. Our inner Goddess is pure and clean and can get uncomfortable when you become a pack rat of negativity; she can get pushed down so far that she barely exists anymore.

What does your laundry room look like when you haven't done laundry for three weeks? It all gets piled up until we are forced to do something about it because we don't have any clean underwear. That's what happens when our lives get stuck and we have nowhere else to turn but inward to finally face a necessary lifetime clean-up. Time to do our inner laundry so our lives get unstuck, flow in a positive direction, and have an unlimited supply of clean undergarments.

Get Your Goddess On!

Our avoidance zone encompasses and affects all of our being. I know for a fact that my Goddess was totally buried in my zone for many years. It's one of the big reasons why I never knew she existed! If I had to speculate as to where this special zone is kept, I'd say it resides in a little known corner of our vast subconscious mind, where we remember everything we want to forget. It's easy to get into and stay in this place. I spent years feeling like it ran my life and I had become its slave.

The worst part is that unfortunately there are unthinkable things people do and say to each other and to themselves every day. As a result, those things go to that place where we cling onto anything negative or heavy because we don't want to deal with them.

This is also the place where we become our mistakes. Our negative self-talk propaganda comes from here and it doesn't matter if any of it is true or not, since we end up believing it anyway. First what you believe about yourself will be all in your head, then eventually manifested in your life somewhere because we want to be right about ourselves. This totally sucks!

Even though this zone is a dark part of us, it's also a place where we have a comfortable chair waiting for us to recline, relax, and replay victim movies of our stories and mistakes, over and over. What a great way to continually remind us of how worthless we are. The place where blame and shame are our best friends. Depression, loneliness, and low self-esteem come often and stay in our guest room for long periods of time. Our avoidance zone is well known, seemingly popular, and unfortunately also welcome in our comfort zone. That's where we can get into trouble.

The Silver Lining

Now for the good news. We can choose something different. We can choose to treat ourselves with more respect and send blame and shame packing. What I discovered on my personal journey of healing is that, if we follow some very simple steps of lessening our load, we can actually get our heads out of this zone and end up with forgiveness and freedom as our best friends instead!

Even though we have years of confirmation invested in our stories and mistakes, it is actually easier to shift out of our avoidance zone than we might think. We may need some help to find a way out, but it might be more helpful to first see how we got into this dark zone.

How Our Avoidance Zone Began

How did we get so comfortable wallowing in our mistakes, our self-pity, and question our worth at every life turn? We've been adding things to this place since before we can remember. Let's go back to the examples and mistakes of the important women in our lives: our mothers, grandmothers, big sisters, aunts, employers, teachers, nuns, and other women of authority when we were growing up. We loved them, admired them, watched them, and often did "monkey see, monkey do" to mimic their behavior.

We saw what worked, and what didn't work, as we grew up because that is what we had in front of us. We formed values and opinions based on our assessment of the good and bad behavior we saw and probably justified their behavior because of the respect we had for our elders.

Keep in mind, when we were little, we didn't have enough maturity or sense of reason to really make good choices. We believed in good faith, that these women were showing us how to do life in the best way possible. Sometimes those role models gave us healthy, positive examples and sometimes not. Regardless of good or bad, we unknowingly modeled our behavior after them anyway.

As children, we were either praised or punished for almost everything we did, based on our family's values. That constant judgment most definitely added to our feelings and perceptions about ourselves. Unfortunately, it seems that the word dysfunction can be used to describe so many families in different ways.

Think about how many nos a child gets versus the number of yeses when they are young. All of these things were parts of our personal avoidance zone that were forming our opinions about ourselves, yet seemed insignificant at the time. Too bad they were far more important than we realized.

Common Yucky

If every woman's story is different and we all have created different paths in life, how is it that so many of us ended up with similar items in our avoidance zones? Many women have feelings of unworthiness, victim mentality, shame, guilt, and blame in our zones. We seem to have a sisterhood that we can relate to each other with a mutual unwritten sympathy. This sisterhood of our common denominators is unfortunately how we also made this dark zone part of our comfort zone as well.

It's too bad that we make ourselves feel right about being comfortable here by continuing to create situations to reinforce what's in our zone. Have you every repeated a mistake over and over? I know I have. We end up doing that because it's what we believe about ourselves, so we are willing to go to the ends of the earth to be right about who we are. And the destructive cycle continues.

To make matters worse, we have shown our daughters, nieces, and students our examples along the way, as if it was okay to live as we live, mistakes and all. If it was good enough for our moms, aunts, grandmas, and us to live a certain way, it must be good enough for our girls. No!

This is the problem since some of us continue to show our daughters how to follow us, even though we sometimes don't even believe in ourselves yet. It's the best way to make sure that the next generation fills up their zone like we did! If you want something else for yourself and the young ladies in your life, then let's go for something new that is behind Door #2.

Fathers and Daughters

There is a misconception that dads automatically have a magical relationship with their daughters. This father–daughter bond can definitely contribute to the success of their daughter's future relationships. I think it's true for some and not true for others. (The same goes for mother–son relationships, so insert whatever your scenario is for this example.)

One of my favorite memories about this phenomenon was from a place of observance one night at a restaurant when I witnessed a father–daughter date at the next table. I had the privilege of sitting next to this beautiful scenario filled with love, respect, and simply wonderful companionship. The dad did all the gentlemanly things for his daughter, complete with pulling the chair out for her and assisting her with ordering (she was just six). I overheard dad asking his daughter questions about her life and what was going on in kindergarten and really listened to her answers. It was magical.

When the little girl went to go to the bathroom, he offered to take her, but she said she was a big girl (and they were only 30 feet from the restroom). I took that opportunity to compliment the dad on such a touching scene. He smiled and said that they have a date once a month. His dad had done something similar with his sisters when he was growing up and he decided to carry on the tradition with his daughter. What fortunate women in that loving family; I was grateful to have witnessed it.

As I left the restaurant, I was unexpectedly emotional. I had never been treated like that as a child and I realized that I had obviously missed this huge piece of relationship 101 groundwork. My father was verbally and emotionally abusive to my mother and all four of us kids in one way or another. I was the middle girl and instead of being taken on father-daughter dates, I had been told on more than one occasion that I "had exceeded his attention span." Now there's a confidence-building statement to tell your seven-year-old daughter.

With every innocent event that unknowingly was abusive, I soon began to bury my Goddess even further, feeling my self-worth crawl down into my zone. Yet, somehow, I had grown to love him anyway and looked past his abusive nature, because he was my dad and it was a form of attention from him. Any attention was better than no attention at that point.

So, in my avoidance zone, I must have held a place of acceptance for abuse in there somewhere. Abuse is just a behavior, not a person—but it is usually associated with a person and comes from within them. My dad was a corporate man and climbed the ladder better than anyone I knew. He didn't have time for us most of our younger years, and I think we all felt it.

The Avoidance Zone

When we did have an occasional game of Frisbee, croquet, a giant water fight, or camping, we ate up every second of that fun side of dad we only saw once in a while. That's where I felt connected to him because that wonderful dad was in there somewhere!

I was fortunate enough to eventually shift my relationship with my dad in several ways before he died. One of those ways was when we got the chance to go out to dinner a couple of times just father and daughter, and I remember it being sweet. I felt cared for, listened to, and very special, just like that little six-year-old girl, even though I was in my mid-30s. He had shifted and so had I. The damage was all but gone inside me, and I was happy to choose another path. A path of love and forgiveness.

I was one of the lucky ones who had the opportunity to re-create that supportive and loving father-daughter date that I had observed years before. I was fortunate to have seen a positive example of what I wanted and had the opportunity to do something about that missing event from my childhood, in the most positive light.

I didn't know it at the time, but that's when I realized that we can do something about all that pile of (you know what) in our avoidance zone. We can choose to rewrite and release whatever we want!

Some dads, like mine, wanted to maintain control over their sons and daughters so they would become obedient children because they were doing as their fathers had done before them. Unfortunately, my dad's father died when he was only thirteen so he had no positive example to follow.

Picture this: my dad was forced to support his mom (a woman who never got her driver's license) while he was in middle school, working two jobs, one before school and one after school, while building

Get Your Goddess On!

a garage and learning how to fix things around the house at the tender age of thirteen. The last part of his childhood was basically robbed from him. Good thing there was no pressure on this kid—no wonder he craved control.

I eventually figured out that his desire for control as he got older came from the fact that he was thrust into a very uncontrollable situation at a very young age. Because of the excess pressures put on him, could all the extra responsibility and frustration have changed who he could have been? I'm guessing yes.

I can only imagine what his zone was filled with, to have become who he was, never being able to act out his anger and frustration about losing his father because he had to be strong for his mom and support her. He hurt inside and eventually that hurt came out on us in different ways because we were there and were easy targets. It's an amazing thing that one single event that happened years before to a young boy could have such a profound influence on my life as I grew up. I'm sorry that I didn't realize this until after he was gone, so I could have cut him some slack when I was growing up.

I feel moms and dads should instill confidence and compassion in their children by their example, not tear them down and create a vast hole of worthlessness that their children spend a lifetime crawling out of. I vote for positive parent–child dates, no matter what the son or daughter combinations are, so we can all learn great respect and appreciation in relationships.

We would have a lot less in our zones if we re-created a new chapter for our relationships with our parents. Let's rewrite us, with a new Goddess twist by being authentic with each other while discarding all of that excess stuff. I will start by saying that as I grew up, so did my dad because we healed together as we both figured life out.

Inventory in the Zone

Let's take Inventory. In our avoidance zone, we have other peoples' examples, memories, our mistakes, and our miscued events we identify with, as well as the lies and stories we have been told and also tell ourselves. You'd think that's enough, but no. It is also filled with other peoples' stuff, too. By believing what other people say about us, or buying into their words or actions toward us, it affects us at our core and gets stored there too.

Here is a secret: *When someone lashes out with actions or words toward you, it's their stuff that they threw at us. It's not our stuff at all!* But we somehow take it in, we believe it, and then wear it as if it's actually who we are, like it was our stuff—but it's not.

When we are clearing our avoidance zone, forgiveness, awareness, and releasing, things sometimes becomes gray. Are we supposed to forgive them for doing or saying what they said, or forgive ourselves for buying into it and believing it? The answer is both.

No matter who or what I'm forgiving as I peel off the layers in this zone, I've discovered that there always seems to be a part of myself to forgive as well. Funny, huh? Forgiving someone else is a beautiful thing. Finding and owning the part I can directly forgive myself for always makes me feel far better when releasing. Keep this in mind as we begin to forgive.

Now, when someone does or says something really foul to me, I stop for a moment to think about how horrible they must feel inside to make them want to say or do what they did. Something horrific must have happened to them somewhere along the way in their life to make them so snarled up inside that what comes out of them is horrible.

Get Your Goddess On!

The key is to realize when it's *their* stuff and not mine, then it never even makes it into my avoidance zone because I never let it get close enough to me to claim it as mine. Send them love and blessings, they need it more than you can imagine—and sending them healing thoughts also helps to diffuse what they have said or done to you.

Taking assessment of our zone inventory is essential and might be pretty emotional. You know darn well what your biggest items are because you don't want to think about them, talk about them, or relive them. They are precisely the ones to deal with first—like eating your lima beans off your plate first. Get it over with.

All of the "lovely" stuff in your avoidance zone has made you who you are today. Embrace it and know that you have control over it now. No longer does it control you. It's only stuff and has nothing whatsoever to do with the magnificent Goddess that you are. Here is something else to ponder as we deal with this yucky and previously avoidable part of life: We can only recognize the light because of the darkness and vice versa. Without that good and bad scenario, we would not appreciate or understand either one of the extremes. If we embrace both dynamics with the gusto they deserve, we will then be one step closer to whole, as we cleanse our past mistakes from our avoidance zone.

Five Action Steps to Lessen the Load: Door #2

Remember the Door #2 that I said I would opt for? This is what is behind Door #2. Here are five steps to use when taking action to empty your avoidance zone. When using these steps, please take on one topic/item at a time. Some bites are huge and some are smaller. Some are related to others and can be convoluted as an underlying theme in all of your zone (for example, mine was abuse). It's also very important to breathe deeply through this process.

It is possible that when doing these steps, emotional garbage will rise to the surface. Breathe through the garbage as well and remember that it is not you, it is just stuff. It is not who you are inside as a Goddess, a being of white light, a sweet soul, and the magnificent person you are on this earth.

Do a little at a time or take on the big ones; your choice. When you need to take a break, stop and allow yourself the time to enjoy the release. If you are anything like me, there could be a lot in there to address—in fact, you could write a whole book on it, like I did.

Let's begin by being in the state of gratitude for the opportunity to handle and release:

1. **Take inventory of your avoidance zone.** What exactly do you not want to think about, talk about, or deal with from your past or present? Make an honest list, as long as it needs to be.

2. **Number this list** from #1 as the worst and go down from there. Remember, you will know the 1 to 3 number items immediately because you *really* don't want to deal with them. The order can change at any time as things come up. It's like making a to-do list or a packing list for a trip—once it's handled, you simply cross it off the list.

3. **Address items by acknowledging them specifically.** These can be situations or abuses that happened to you or you did to someone else. Do one at a time and separate out the list with identification and awareness. Seek further

clarification of things so you can see the real problem that is at the root in the zone—dig deep to see what is on the bottom of the pile that is negatively affecting you in your life. It helped me to write one sentence to describe each item on my list, or it could be a whole paragraph or a page.

4. **Divide out their stuff and your stuff** as you create the realization of what the situation was, words that were used to hurt you or that you hurt others with, abusive actions or words. Color code these with a highlighter if you choose.

5A. **Deal with *their stuff* first.** Clean it out first because it's easily recognizable now and gets you into the practice and rhythm of dealing with you next. Put these items in the category of life lesson for the next time someone throws their stuff at you. Keep in mind who was involved, what you learned, and how you benefited from it in any way. Let it go because it's not yours anyway. Thank them (in your head) for the lesson.

5B. **Own up to *your stuff*,** cry as much as you need to, and make it right with yourself and someone else if you need to. You don't have to physically do or say anything to another person. It could be done silently in a meditation-like way, let them know what you want them to understand or forgive about the situation or action through your thoughts. Be vulnerable with yourself and remember the lesson. This is where the real magic happens!

Do this exercise as often as you need to. When you complete any session, take a general inventory again and celebrate any and all reductions in your zone. Embrace your Goddess within and thank her for her help! Cross things off your list as you go. Breathe. Remain in a state of gratitude as you work through this process. Be grateful for the lessons, for lightening your load of burden, and for the freedom each release brings.

It's time to sit quietly and assess where you are with your inner self, your Goddess space, and reflect on your journey so far. My hope for you is that your cleansing has been a positive experience and your introspective efforts have been rewarded. We're near the end of our grueling cleansing adventure and the party is about to begin. Answer your questions with your heart to complete your awareness and prepare to get to know your Goddess. Breathe.

Chapter 6 Questions

1. Take Inventory and do the five-step exercise above for one hot issue. Be specific and honest with yourself to get better results in lessening your load! Repeat as necessary. There are extra sheets in the back of the book to use if needed.

_____

_____

_____

_____

_____

_____

_____

Get Your Goddess On!

_____
_____
_____

2. Describe how you will feel when your avoidance zone is empty and everything has been handled. Now go do it!

_____
_____
_____
_____
_____
_____
_____
_____
_____
_____
_____
_____
_____
_____

CHAPTER SEVEN

The Story of My Forgiveness

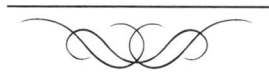

Congratulations! Open your heart and love yourself because your party is about to begin. Everything is ready and the atmosphere you have prepared is magical. It's now time to enjoy your Goddess and what you have created.

Forgiveness is the most amazing gift you can give or receive. The reason for forgiveness is for you to lighten your load when you acknowledge, own, then release. It allows your disposition to heal, as well as your life, your outlook, and your spirit, and it enhances your dreams! It can also help you to see and *own* your Goddess and to realize that you have her within you always!

The coolest part about forgiveness is that there is no time limit, expiration date, waiting time, or line to stand in—it is available 24/7/365, always at your service.

For many years, I thought forgiveness was all about forgiving others. What I didn't realize is that forgiving me was the most important thing I could do for myself. It's almost impossible to forgive others if you don't know how to forgive yourself, which is why resentment and grudges are rampant with so many people. Regularly practicing self-forgiveness is by far the healthiest state to be in; but, if you are like me, I had no idea how to get there without losing myself in the process.

Here's why: For most of my life, I had this unhealthy idea that forgiveness was only about someone else and it meant that I was letting them off the hook. It meant also that they got away with something that hurt me. I had to give in, to forgive them, even if they were the one that was totally wrong. How could this be a good thing? I had seen many people in my life hold grudges and pretend to forgive, but I don't remember seeing true forgiveness.

When we were young and I was told to forgive my sister, I heard my obligatory "sorry," I said, "I forgive you," and then we went on playing. My siblings and I traded those same pretend words back and forth for our entire childhood because mom told us we had to. I never really quite knew what it meant to forgive or how to do it past those few words.

My position was to automatically accept someone's apology, then move on like nothing happened, even if I knew they didn't mean it. Sadly, these two tiny paragraphs encompass my total knowledge of forgiveness when I was young.

Then life started to get more complicated when relationships entered the picture. I got my heart broken, I broke someone else's heart, and the cycle continued over and over. Of course, it didn't occur to me that there was anything to forgive in myself, but I sure saw many things in other people that needed some help. I became good at justifying my behavior and was miserable from holding onto all this stuff and pretending everything was fine on the outside so no one knew.

The Story of My Forgiveness

Forgiveness was still pretty foreign to me going into adulthood, and somehow I ended up twisting things around again, thinking that I should be the one who needed to be more thoughtful or congenial, no matter who was at fault. My goal was to make the confrontation in front of me go away; I really just wanted to be liked in the end for doing everything I could to make everything work. Is this a good time to mention that I was a middle child and raised in a Catholic school?

At one point in my life I was struggling with a career path, I felt like nothing I did mattered, and I was in a relationship that drained me of all joy. I was in the middle of a pile of crap and there were no other footsteps but my own on the path to get there! Something had to change to get something different and unfortunately no one was volunteering to do it for me.

A well-meaning friend suggested I start to meditate to see if I could get to the bottom of why I felt so unsuccessful in life. I did it begrudgingly at first, then I got it and heard my answer loud and clear: I needed to begin by forgiving myself first. There is a well-known secret that needs to be repeated.

There is one person who needs the most forgiveness you can muster. She is amazingly unaware that she has really screwed up. She is also oblivious to the fact that she is connected to every single thing in your avoidance zone. You are in fact the #1 person who needs your forgiveness.

Forgiveness Discovery

Forgiveness has been written about in as many ways as there are books on the subject. What I found out about forgiveness didn't seem to be enough, so I added an element that offered the responsibility I needed. I didn't always want to face what I had to forgive in myself, but the byproduct was a short cut to my Goddess. I found authenticity and personal freedom within the process of forgiveness, when I faced all of me and added that ownership step in the middle.

Adopting self-forgiveness as a part of your daily life is one of the healthiest choices you can make. Adding love, joy, clarity, and heaps of gratitude to the quality of your life definitely makes it worth the effort.

If you haven't spent much time forgiving yourself, now is the perfect time to start. By completing the cleansing of your internal house, you can feel lighter and enjoy getting rid of more junk. Once I discovered this, I was literally on the verge of becoming a forgiveness junkie because the more I did, the more I wanted.

There's a reason why there is so much baggage piled around you. Picture each piece of baggage with someone's name, date, or event on it that you don't want to deal with. If your life isn't working as well as you'd like, take a look at who is sitting in the middle of the excessive pile of this baggage. If you are tired of feeling bogged down, then start removing the heavy layers in your zone by dealing with one piece at a time!

The Three-Step Self-Forgiveness Process

Let's start with some key words:

ACKNOWLEDGE: To make known that something or someone is real; words describing what is.

OWN: (Responsibility) Having absolute authority or full claim of possession: It's mine!

RELEASE: To fully let go of something freely, resulting in joy, clarity, and freedom.

Step One: Acknowledge what it is that needs to be forgiven. State the basics of what is going on. No blame, no embellished stories, just the facts, ma'am! Think of it as a generic description.

Step Two: Own what your part *and* identify the other person's parts in the event. What are you each responsible for? Use an "I" statement to take responsibility for what you know to be true about yourself. It's crucial for you to really get this before moving on to Release. This was the piece that was missing for me in all the other processes I came across.

Step Three: Release it! Forgive who for what and especially *yourself*. You can only let go of what you now own! Be in gratitude and say "Thank you!"

Sounds pretty simple, doesn't it? It is. The fact that I could always connect myself somehow to everything I was forgiving shocked me. Why? Because I didn't like being responsible for even a little bit of it because blame was easier and much more fun. When I discovered that piece, that's when I could finally release. Before I added all three of these steps, I was only pretending to release—that's why it wasn't doing much. (Did I forget to mention again that this requires taking responsibility?)

At times, the only thing I saw to forgive myself for was tolerating the other person's behavior, or allowing this person to be in my life when I knew they were trouble. This may seem trivial, but it is important to acknowledge because it was still taking even a small piece of responsibility. By looking deep to see what part I played, it created those magical little pockets of freedom. Sometimes it was so simple and pretty obvious, other times it was buried deep in the story.

Ownership is the tricky step and is also what made the difference for me. Here's an example I like to use to explain this step. If I'm at my friend's house and I borrow a shirt from her to go out. I wear it, then take it home and wash it. Can I then give it away to my favorite resale shop? No. Why? Because it's not mine. I can't give away something I don't own.

Ownership is more personal, is much more specific, and is usually where you find the things you don't want to admit about yourself. The more you personalize it, the more you can actually see exactly what you are releasing.

You will know if you forgive completely, because when you release, you will feel free of that burden and a shift from blame because it won't matter anymore. Another reason I originally felt incomplete when I released stuff is because I kept ownership of my actions at an arm's length away, so it didn't work. Open your eyes, heart, and head during this process and ask your Goddess for help. Fully releasing is worth any effort you put into it.

I am happy to be wrong about my old ideas of forgiveness. It wasn't about letting them off the hook or allowing them to get away with something. It is about how that "thing" I was forgiving was controlling me. I was also comforted because it doesn't require any forgetting in the process, so you still get to keep the lesson for future reference. Think of it like a file cabinet in the basement: you only go there when you absolutely need something from it.

I say keep the lesson, throw away the wrapper, but remember what the label looked like for the next time you want it. In other words, forgive, learn, remember, and move on. This has been the best preventative tool I've found for my "repeating my mistakes" issue!

Testing the System: Operation Art School Revisited

Let's revisit my favorite family example of the need to forgive. The scene is set in the family room in the afternoon, with an orange Formica bar, dark paneling around the room, extremely worn green and orange shag carpeting, and those horrible words swirling around the room.

No wonder I became a decorator—that room left some pretty visual scars—maybe it's when I unconsciously decided to rescue the world from whatever that was. I couldn't help it. My psyche etched the scene in my memory because there were undeniable emotional, mental, psychological, and physical components to the conversation.

To come clean with you, I still hadn't forgiven my dad for moving us up from my fun-filled Mississippi house a year and a half ago. There, we had an in-ground pool in the back yard, a one-block walk to the Gulf of Mexico and its beautiful sandy beach, sunshine, and lots of great friends, and of course my cheerleading squad. I was still really ticked.

So where in that scenario did that man deserve to be forgiven? Nowhere, in my opinion. What I didn't know is that by not dealing with the blame, I was cutting myself short of any chance of happiness. I was still holding a grudge and had unknowingly given my power to him long ago, along with my joy and sense of reason because I was so stuck in resentment. (Remember the definition of resentment is taking poison, then waiting for the other person to die, haha!)

Get Your Goddess On!

It eventually dawned on me how one little act of forgiveness with my father and myself could have changed my life years ago and made it so much more fulfilling and free. Hindsight stings sometimes.

The forgiveness was totally for me in the end. It's sad, looking back at the time I wasted by holding onto everything and fueling it for years. Imagine if I had put all that energy and intent into something positive and productive. I could have gotten out of that pathetic pity party long before that and gained my freedom sooner. Even though he was gone by the time I did this, it only mattered that I forgave; I trust that he heard me in heaven.

Did you know that family can be the #1 area filling your avoidance zone and may hold the deepest wounds since our families form our first memories and can sometimes affect us the rest of our lives, both good and bad. Think about the top 10 things you have on your list to forgive, and I'll bet there are four or more in the category of parents/siblings/family. You've heard family comes first—I'm now saying it is second in the forgiveness line, after ourselves.

Let's put the story of forgiving my dad and the process together to see how easy it is to work through. This process works the same on everything big or small that you need to forgive.

Step One: Acknowledge: I wanted to go to art school. My father disagreed and had other ideas. I didn't have enough funds to branch out on my own, and I needed parental support. I ended up having to go into a field that he wanted me to go into instead of art. I was bummed.

Step Two: Own: My father was really just being a pain in the ass parent by wanting to control my life to protect me and make sure I had a great life. Even though he did it in a horrible way, he actually did it out of love and support for me. His dad died when he was very young so he never had anyone looking out for him like this. He could have found another way of saying this, but he never really did know how to sugar-coat anything.

I blew it when I drank too much at a party in my senior year, and it fueled his concern about alcohol and artists. Who knows, they may have supported me in an art-related field if I hadn't done that. I also dropped the ball and didn't put a plan together or save enough money to go to art school to follow my dream.

What I had done was assume parental support, instead of planning for my future. Since I didn't act like I knew how to put my future together, Dad stepped in and did it for me. I should have been more assertive with my life and been more proactive instead of such a free spirit when it came to my future.

Step Three: Release: I forgave Dad for choosing my career for me and how it changed my life path because I appreciated his dedication to me and my future by doing what he thought was best for me, even though it was hard for me to hear. He did the best he could at the time.

I forgave myself for drinking too much at that party—I was totally out of line. I don't blame him for being harsh about it, since I already knew it was a sensitive subject for him and I know that I really scared and disappointed both my parents that night they had to pick me out of the bushes after I passed out.

I also forgave myself for going along with his plan without any further effort on my part toward what I really wanted to do. I failed to plan ahead and I learned too late to stand up for myself, but I'm thankful that planning is now a way of life for me. Thank you!

Get Your Goddess On!

NOTE: You can choose to do all your forgiveness on paper in your notes, in a letter, in your head, in person, or combinations of all four ways. This is your forgiveness process—make it your own.

After the Process

The rest of this story is that I am grateful for my amazingly positive life results. My life turned out to be very creative after all. Art may or may not have supported me in my career, but it actually doesn't matter. The whole thing is yesterday's breakfast at this point.

One of the strongest places my Goddess shows up is in my creativity everywhere in my life. It makes me tick. Many times when I feel at my very best, I am creating in the garden, in my studio, writing at my computer, or in a client's home incorporating artistic expression into everything I do. A few of the ways I kept my art within me are the following:

1. I taught papermaking at an art museum for two years, and evening classes in mosaics at a local home décor store for about a year and a half. I achieved my goal in becoming a teacher!

2. I was artist in residence for a grade school for many weeks. Hundreds of kids called me Miss Cat for several weeks and I really got to be a teacher here!

3. My business is all about creating a look for people in their homes and gardens, every day.

4. I continue to create art in several mediums all my life, sharing my passion with my talented daughters, students, and girlfriends.

Another bonus that came out of this event was that I gave all my children the opposite opportunity I was given. They were all able to choose whatever they wanted to do in life. I promised them the freedom, have supported their wishes, and given them opportunities in life that I only dreamed of. By giving them what I didn't have, the freedom to choose, it felt good. My youngest child is going through the pre-college process right now; she's ready and so am I.

I feel like I am finally living my dream, too, by taking more pride in working toward my goals in life, becoming a better, happier, and more successful version of what I once was. I had to learn the hard way I guess, but in the end, it made my victories that much sweeter when I achieved my goals with perseverance, dedication, and lots of reinventing myself.

What Else I Learned

I eventually forgave my father again and again when I became a parent, because I realized how much I had contributed greatly to his fearful behavior toward me in that fateful conversation. He was operating out of fear for me and decided this was the best way to "scare me straight," and I couldn't blame him for making that choice out of love for me.

Was it the right choice? It really doesn't matter now. What does matter is the lesson I took away from the experience. My parents both loved me, even though he just chose a less than stellar way to show me my lesson. That was who he was.

My lesson? I am responsible for me. If I'm not going to be responsible for me, then someone will step in and assume the role and make whatever choices for me that they want to, without consulting me. I like it better if I'm the one in charge. Amazingly simple lesson, yet so far away for so many years.

Just imagine if I had actually been smart by saving money, avoided binge drinking, and did my homework as to career options with possible salaries before our college conversation. I know I would've enhanced my future instead of putting it behind the eight ball. No wonder he was so callused! I was fortunate that he cared so much, but sure wished he had buffered the conversation a lot more than he did—but he didn't so he could get my attention. He sure did.

The choice my father made was small in comparison as to what I chose to do with it. Forgiving him was actually the easy part in the end because I understood his intentions. Taking the responsibility for not taking responsibility allowed me the freedom I needed to fully forgive him and resulted in letting go of so many of those self-worth issues immediately.

Hindsight says that if I had been smarter before the conversation, it would have been a totally different, positive conversation and he wouldn't have felt the need to make decisions for me. But I wouldn't have this great story and years of anguish to add to this book, so I'm not sure what would have been better. (Ha ha!) The end result was that I let it go and got to enjoy my parents in new, more meaningful ways for many years before he died.

They both actually ended up working for me for several years in the first start-up company I was a part of! I think that having your father work for your company after he told you that you won't be successful is one of the definitions of karma . . . I love karma.

The Forgiveness Plan

It is a glorious choice to forgive. The question now is, how will you use your newfound knowledge? It would be beneficial to examine your own beliefs about forgiveness first. In the beginning, I was certainly barely open to any type of forgiveness and when I pretended to do it on the surface, it didn't work.

The Story of My Forgiveness

Forgive, learn, remember, and move on is one of my favorite parts of this chapter. This process changed my life in every way imaginable; I hope it does the same for you! Put a plan together of who, what, where, why, and how you will forgive and remember to put yourself on that list!

When Horrible Things Happen

There are times when horrible things may happen to you, where you become the victim of an unthinkable event. It's too surreal to imagine that you have anything to forgive in yourself when that happens. I know because I have been there. It took me 22 years to say that.

In fact, I wrote a poem about my unthinkable event and I've shared it here with you. I added this very personal part of my life to demonstrate my level of vulnerability and commitment to your healing process. During my journey, I noticed that there was still a slightly open space within me from this past event. When I wrote "The Moon," I filled that little piece of darkness with pure, divine, white light in the form of words.

Originally, when I wrote this, forgiveness was the last thing I was thinking about because I had worked through so much of everything already. In the end, it came to the surface so naturally in the telling of the story and it made all the difference, giving me one of the last unknown pieces of the puzzle.

Forgiveness of the unthinkable events in life works exactly the same as the simple and easy things when using the forgiveness process. You first must choose forgiveness though, in order for success to be yours. Using compassionate thoughts and honest efforts in the releasing process of your event is important to remember when forgiving such things. It can be done.

Get Your Goddess On!

The Moon
By Cat Dols

The lesson was learned,
even though the student was unwilling at first.
It was not what she signed up for,
or so she thought.

In May of 1979,
The first weekend,
She felt disconnected for quite some time,
but still she wanted to see him.
College was almost over.
Real life was about to begin,
Whatever real life is.

Bus ride was bumpy from Point A to Point B,
and so were her thoughts.
The plan was to do it smoothly,
without problems.
Without fighting,
Without him hating her,
And still be friends.
Ha . . .

The ride seemed longer,
Her thoughts got clearer.
It would HAVE to be this weekend.
He met her at the bus station,
and seemed happy at first,
to see each other.

Time for the talk.
No time for that.

The Story of My Forgiveness

Time for bands on campus
and beer flowing on a sunny afternoon.
Let's Dance!
Did I mention it was Friday?

Maybe it would still work,
the two of them.
Maybe the connection would rekindle,
Maybe he would seem like he cared again,
Maybe the Moon was made out of cheese . . .

Then to the Dorms to prepare for the night out
at the square.
Let's drink some more.
Let's really numb our senses,
And truths would be forgotten . . .
And all would be perfect (again?).
And the Moon really would be made out of cheese.

The conversation began.
The beer already in their veins.
Lots more in his because he started earlier
Less in hers because she had something to say.
It was time to say good bye,
Even though he was still her dream.
It didn't feel the same anymore.
He didn't fill her needs.
It didn't seem too much to ask,
To live in separate ways.
His rage was Huge.
His pride stunned.
His beer spoke in harsh tones.
His eyes lit on fire.
His hands clenched with hatred.
The words couldn't be taken back.

Get Your Goddess On!

They were on the table, on the rug, on the bedspread,
In the air of the room.

No, thank you—no more partying,
She didn't care for any more fun,
and would leave in the morning.
Can't imagine why.
Three and a half years were now reduced to done.
When did it slip away from them?
Must've been when life got busy living.
Another lesson learned,
It was nice to have it over,
Or so she thought.

He left her and said they could talk again when he returned.
He wouldn't be long.
He said, "Be here when I get back,
there's more to say."
He just didn't say what way he would say it.
Oh good, she thought,
There's a chance we could still be friends,
and work this out.
There's a chance the Moon really is made out of cheese!

His vacated roommate's bed available,
Looked like the perfect place to sleep,
'till our conversation continued . . .
Not all communication is verbal you know.
She had the chance to leave for four hours.
Silly, Silly Girl . . .
Her head was filled with fluff like Pooh Bear.
Her heart just still wanted to be liked.
Silly, Silly Girl . . .

And all the while the silly girl slept,

The Story of My Forgiveness

The angry boy drank beer.
Oh, how he must have looked forward to
the rest of their conversation.
As she fell asleep,
she looked forward too.
Surely it would go well.
Surely he would see her point and be gracious.

Bar time came.
He walked in and looked at the silly girl,
asleep on his roommate's bed.
What did he want to say to her?
He wanted to tell her how he felt.
What better way than to show her,
So he turned the mattress over on her.
He shoved his weight on top.
He heard her cry.
He heard her pain.

He knew she was still breathing.
Oh, maybe a pillow would work better.
Nobody breaks up with him he says . . .
Thank God for built-in desks in dorms!
The mattress hit the edge.
The pillow couldn't reach enough to smother her.
The surprise attack and damage was done.
Her tailbone cracked with the first hit to the floor.
How could he do this to her?

Yet it wasn't enough.
More was in store for the silly girl who stayed.
Arms and legs pulled and bruised as she fought.
Hair yanked and wet with tears.
Excruciating pain in her lower back.
It can't get any worse.

Get Your Goddess On!

Or so she thought.

Held down on the bed,
She couldn't move.
Her pain encompassed all of her being.
This couldn't be happening.
He ripped off anything that was on her.
He entered her harshly, without permission.
She said no and fought him
He hit her.
She cried.
He called her names,
Bad ones.
Then he passed out, thank God.
Not before saying,
She should remain
Or he would hunt her down.
She never dreamed of being in this way.

She crawled out from under the monster somehow.
She vomited because of the shock.
She peed in a trashcan in the corner,
for fear he'd wake up and find her gone.
He had taught her a lesson alright.
Now what was she to do with it from here?

In the morning, he begged her to stay.
In the morning, she said no.
Staying with someone out of fear was no way to live she said.
She was twenty.
Now she started to be smart.
He didn't like her being smart and started screaming,
And hit her across the face.
So hard it left a hand mark for a week on her cheek.
He was left handed.

The Story of My Forgiveness

As she crawled to the door to escape,
He threw things at her.
Now her ribs were bruised too,
as she raised her hands to protect her swollen face.
He screamed at her.
The door was hers.
It opened.
She found a new friend in the hall.
This new friend called for more new friends.
They seemed to like her when they saw her.
They really wanted to help.
He came out the door after her,
Grabbing her arm to pull her back in.
Her new friends said no.
Instead her new friends grabbed his arms
And held him down.

Making new friends had never been so sweet.
She lay there from exhaustion.
Her new friends took him down the hall to another room.
Where he went was not important.
Where she was going was.
She collected her things.
She couldn't walk very well.
It was raining.
She had 37 offers to drive her to the bus station.
She turned down all 37.
She felt the urge to rescue herself.
To walk out on her own two feet.
It was part of the lesson.
She limped to the bus and propped herself up in a seat.
And she cried all the way home.

When she got home,
She hid her roommates' keys before she told them.

Get Your Goddess On!

But she didn't have to tell them.
They could see the marks and the bruises already.
And they could see the pain in her eyes.
Three sweet gentlemen and three ladies in the house.
She was like a sister.
They finally promised her they would not go.
She was held and nurtured.
She healed and cried.
She told very few until now.

She never told her dad or brother the whole truth,
to keep them from going to jail, of course.
She kept the burden to herself,
For you see his mom was ill.
If it came out, it could have killed her.
No, it's better tucked away,
To eat at her insides.
Until 30 years later,
When she helped a young girl
With a similar lesson.
Maybe it happened to her for a reason,
She thought.
Maybe she could teach others about this lesson.
Maybe she has a story to tell,
So other girls won't be so silly,
And their heads wouldn't be filled with fluff.
A way of helping that she never dreamed of before.

One thing she knows for sure,
Is the time she had to leave,
Was the time she just wanted to be liked,
And to fix things with this boy.
Silly, Silly Girl.
Now she knows to teach others about
How to be smart girls!

Another thing she knows for sure,
Is that the gift of life lessons sometimes come in funny packages,
without bows.
Teaching others about these lessons and how to avoid them
Is a good step.
Now she knows to help heal others with her words.
Maybe she was chosen for this lesson
because it made her stronger and smarter.

And now she knows that there is absolutely no way the Moon is
made out of cheese.

The Conversation

"She felt the urge to rescue herself," is my favorite line in the poem. I think that will always be one of the top five experiences of my life. Not the rape, but the moment I chose to own my power in the face of excruciating adversity. In the end, what happened to me was not as important as what I did with the experience.

I wrote "The Moon" thirty years after that fateful weekend, and it was created as a result of a simple conversation with my 18-year-old daughter after she qualified for state in high school forensics. (Poetry reading, not dead bodies!) She was looking for something amazing to "wow" the judges with and thought my experience would create the emotional impact she was looking for.

The back story is that many years ago, after I came to terms with 98% of my personal hell, I shared my experience with my children in the form of a learning moment. I also let them know that I put very little importance on this once traumatic event, choosing to define myself with more positive and loving ways of being. Even though I had let that one single event define me at one time, I was no longer being held hostage by it. I showed them that I am bigger than "it."

Get Your Goddess On!

The conversation I am about to describe was not your average mother-daughter Tuesday evening chit chat about skirt lengths or curfews. I gave it the simple importance of an everyday opportunity for a mother to help her child with a request, nothing more, nothing less. It had taken me many years to work through all the facets of being raped and beaten up by someone I knew and who supposedly loved me. I realized that I was totally on the other side, so to speak, when I was able to candidly have this conversation.

> **Daughter:** Mom, I'm reading a poem for State and I want it to be really emotional. Can you please write a poem about when you were raped and beaten up in college?
>
> **Mom:** Sure, honey, when do you need it?
>
> **Daughter:** On Thursday or before. [It's Tuesday night.]
>
> **Mom:** Well, I'll at least see if I can put an outline or something together by then, okay? And how long does it need to be?
>
> **Daughter:** Oh, eight minutes . . . and thanks Mamma.

In your wildest dreams, could you *ever* imagine having that conversation with anyone, let alone your 18-year-old daughter? I sat down that night with the intention of an outline. What I produced, after just two hours of writing, was this exact poem, which took me (you guessed it) eight minutes to read. I have kept it virtually intact since the moment I wrote it in the spring of 2009. With an irregular writing style that is haphazard and free, I'm pretty sure the poem will never win any prizes or awards. I'm okay with it simply being used as a teaching tool. It has really been for my eyes only until now. (Follow-up note: This was never read at any forensics competition because we found out later that the topic was taboo with the organization.)

I knew I needed help writing about an event such as this in a healthy yet vulnerable way as I relived the experience, while staying detached. No problem. I called upon my inner child, a familiar inner source of power that is part of my Goddess, and who has always been available to assist me. My inner child remains that magic age of seven, when I was both vulnerable and confident at the same time. That night I asked her to help me write from a third-person point of view. I needed to tell my story through the eyes of a child to keep it G-rated for the audience at State and somehow I felt safer with her on my team that night.

And then I began to write. And I cried. And I wrote some more, I cried some more, and then I read it. Bingo! Mission accomplished! I said thank you to my inner child for her assistance, feeling like I had just released the weight of the world. With puffy eyes and feeling emotionally wiped out, I had written a poem on a stained yellow legal pad that allowed me to heal even more than I thought was possible. It was cathartic. I must have finally been ready to write it. "The Moon" ultimately is about realization and forgiveness, but not for the reasons I had originally thought. Healing words made for a healing heart.

Clean Up, Clean Up, Every Woman Everywhere . . .

One of the things I did as I began my journey to love myself was to do some seriously major cleaning up, inside and out. Imagine again, taking care of yourself like you take care of your car. If you are meticulous in the care of your vehicle, it lasts longer and keeps

Get Your Goddess On!

its value. If you don't take care of the structure of any system, it starts to deteriorate immediately regardless if it's a car, house, or a person. A good portion of this book ended up being about this cleansing process and is actually how I left the darkness and walked into the light.

After my realization, on the inside I found self-forgiveness and the power of healing through writing. I hadn't written a poem in 32 years, and I was so surprised that it totally changed my life by allowing me to heal even more than I thought was possible. The words just flowed out, the emotions, ideas, and thoughts blending together on the page like a watercolor palette. The images that they portrayed were raw, yet safe somehow.

My special cleansing process happened to be a poem, then eventually a book to help others. Your form could be a journal, a short story, a question and answer format, scrapbooking, photography, video, song writing, or another creative process that you are comfortable with.

As I let the words spill out onto the paper, I had a chance to step away from the situation and realize that by being so incredibly congenial that night, it almost cost me my life. I am grateful to be alive.

If I had just paid attention to the signs of his temper, his anger, his words, and actions, I could have left to go to the bus station just after he went out to the bars. It was such an obvious opportunity for me and I didn't even realize it *fully* until I stepped away and cleansed one of the last little parts I had left untouched for over 22 years.

> **I forgave myself for staying in the room when I could have left for four hours. That was what was holding me back in life and the key to my freedom**

from that horrific experience. I had the ability to prevent this unthinkable event, but my naïve ways kept me there because I didn't want to hurt his feelings and I still wanted to be liked. How sad.

Another simple thing to forgive in myself was for believing that I somehow deserved this treatment, just because he told me so. When I stopped treating myself that way, it made a profound difference in who I became.

I started taking much better care of myself in every physical manner. I also treated myself with more kindness and respect. I really mattered to me and believed in myself, embracing my newfound confidence. My intentions of healthier eating, exercising, positive life habits, and emotional freedom were obviously a re-dedication to my health through my caring actions.

I began to talk about the event, too. In the several self-help courses I took over the years, there were opportunities to work with a partner or in small groups on many occasions. There was no accident that in one of the exercises, I was partnered with a young woman who shared her story with me. She had been through a similar experience several months before. We created the time and space in that brief partnership to heal together because of our common secret that we now talked about. It was beautiful and empowering for both of us.

The true beauty is that she was able to have a very accountable conversation with the big questions in a matter of months after her event, not decades. I was grateful to help her with my voice and knowledge. Will I ever know what the true reason I experienced being raped was really for? Probably not. Nonetheless, I have embraced helping others as a way to make sense of it all.

Get Your Goddess On!

On this journey to find my own Goddess, I found out that I had to be vulnerable sometimes, especially in the beginning. To get to my core inside, I needed to really look, dig deep, and be totally honest with myself. I had to discover the truth of why I had such a hard time authentically living and forgiving and instead creating chaos in my life. To get to the bottom of what was holding me back, why I kept repeating my mistakes and why couldn't I be honest with myself, I had to learn all the ways I had given my power away. This experience was a biggie.

It was one of those major game changers for me. In the realization of what I was doing to continually sabotage myself, I could then recognize how to heal with forgiveness and create my own personal awareness. It's time to clean yourself up and become the Goddess that you were meant to be!

Note: I want to address something else unthinkable, in case anyone is thinking about how I addressed forgiveness with my event. It is never a child's fault, in any way, if they are attacked and sexually abused. Innocence in children is sacred and to be preserved at all costs. The only thing I can ever imagine a child forgiving themselves for in these cases is believing that in any way that they deserved the horrible treatment that someone did to them. They did not.
oxox

The Rest of the Story

The same daughter who asked me to write the poem many years ago was looking at colleges later that month. She did not know the actual college where this event took place, because I never told her. She just so happened to pick that same college to tour as she had narrowed it down to two different schools. I chose to remain silent about the school before the visit.

The Story of My Forgiveness

While on the college tour, I got a phone call, so I stayed outside the building for a moment to talk. I hurried to catch up with the group that had already gone in to see a sample dorm room. Since we had come from the side of the building, I didn't realize which dorm we were going into. Most of the group had already gone through when I entered the building and saw which dorm we were in.

Much to my surprise, instead of the first floor, we went to another floor, the room down the hall, on the left, before the stairway . . . oh my, could this be real? I was alone in the narrow hallway. The rest of the group had already gone on, heading down the stairs to the next stop on the tour.

There I stood in the doorway of the room I had escaped from at the age of 20.

My Goddess held me sweetly. I quietly faced my fears as I peered into the room that I crawled from one sunny Saturday morning in May, with the help of my new friends. The room was beautiful. It was now a girls' floor. I was numb. Was this some kind of cruel joke?

They were very neat girls, the colors were soothing, and it smelled like lily of the valley. Then something wonderful happened: I smiled as tears streamed down my cheeks and I said, "thank you" to the room. I had survived the ordeal partly because the room had helped save me when the mattress hit the desk. It was so much smaller than I remembered and I was grateful that the room took such good care of me.

After all, I wasn't sure that night, if I would have lived to tell my story. I immediately went to an image in my mind a scene from *Casablanca* when Humphrey Bogart's character says something about all the gin joints in all the world, you had to walk into mine . . . yes, Bogey, I feel you.

Get Your Goddess On!

The room had healed too and was obviously taking very good care of the new girls. When I caught up to my daughter and the group of moms and kids, I did not realize that I still had streaming tears of joy down my cheeks. My daughter asked what was wrong and I told her that the room we just saw, was the one I had been raped in in 1979 . . .

I didn't realize there was anyone else there with us, kind of in a zone. The three nearby women gasped and were in shock. Then, at lunch, they asked me to tell them (and their daughters) about the experience, I guess to learn from it. What a lovely gift they gave me, to be able to share my lesson with them.

I have no idea if I ever prevented any one of those girls from having a similar event, but if they had knowledge after I told my story, then my lesson was for a teaching purpose. I'd like to think I helped those young girls become smarter that day. Better smarter than silly and naïve. The unexpected visit to that room and the healing that occurred by seeing it again was the last 1%. I healed 100% that day and my heart grew 10 times bigger.

Time Changes Things

In 1979, there were no such thing as personal computers or cell phones, and texting hadn't even been thought of yet. I feel a bit foolish, but the only reason I went up to that college to break up with this bad boyfriend was because I wanted my artwork back. He had several of my favorite pieces in his dorm room, so a phone call wouldn't have been enough.

That was my first mistake, staying in the room was my second, and letting it all eat at me for 22 years was my third mistake. A mistake trifecta! All because my high school clay projects were so damn

The Story of My Forgiveness

important to me—seems pathetic when I think about it now. It's ironic that I left most of them there as I walked out.

Actually, for the cheap cost of the bus ticket, the trip had quite a hefty price tag in the end. To tally up, it included being beaten up, raped, a cracked tailbone, bloodshot eyes, cracked ribs, a dislocated jaw, chunks of hair missing, many, many scratches and bruises, humiliation, and of course the emotional scars and memories to destroy all my self-esteem, dignity, and self-worth for years to come. If I had only known the real price of the trip, I may have searched for an easier way to break up with him and considered my art a lost cause from the beginning.

Just think, with today's technology, it could have been handled much more efficiently by texting him after I left a voicemail message (to break up). Then I could have followed it up with changing my status on social media, along with an email detailing the reasons for feeling it was best we break up and listing the artwork as well as attaching some photos of the pieces I wanted back.

Then, I would have found a way to make some new clay pieces to replace the original ones when he refused to give them back to me . . . oh, the technological advancements we've made that make life so much simpler today!

At the time of my original quest for healing, I actually had no idea that any part of me was Goddess-like. I think if I were to visualize my Goddess, mine would have looked like a beautiful white Christmas angel, with a purely angelic face of a cherub, but sitting in a bucket all covered in maple syrup, unable to move, or be recognized as anything other than a dark glob in a bucket.

Get Your Goddess On!

That's how weighed down I felt living, eating, breathing, and sleeping deep dark unworthiness. I truly didn't realize I had a way out until I really forgave myself and started to regain my power.

Now go enjoy your party—this is where the real fun begins!

Chapter 7 Questions

1. What are your beliefs and experiences with forgiveness?

_____
_____
_____
_____
_____
_____
_____
_____
_____

2. Tell your story. (Yes, that one.)

   The Three-Step Self-Forgiveness Process

   Acknowledge: _____
   _____

The Story of My Forgiveness

Own: _____

_____

_____

Release: _____

_____

_____

3. List your top five things/people/events for you to forgive (including yourself). Use extra pages in the back of the book and do the exercise for each of the items on your list.

_____

_____

_____

_____

_____

_____

_____

_____

_____

_____

_____

Get Your Goddess On!

4. Write about your most traumatic or meaningful experience and ask for help within. Use a short story, poem, journal entry, photograph, sketches, or any other creative method to convey your experience. Share your lessons when you are ready.

CHAPTER EIGHT

Authentic Goddess Relationships

The "getting to know her" phase of your Goddess journey is in full swing at your life party. How you show up is important and sets the authentic tone of your relationship with yourself. It's time to pay attention to you now and really enjoy every minute. You have done the work to cleanse and now you're in the building and learning phase of new relationships in your life, starting with your Goddess. Go mingle around your life party and enjoy your personal power like an old friend who has just arrived.

Another key to your journey is being truly authentic. This sucks because we've already established that no one really wants to be accountable for every little thing they do, if they don't have to. Authenticity is sometimes a tougher path because of it, but in the end it's worth it to have an amazing life that produces byproducts like joy, presence, and the ability to live within your power!

Get Your Goddess On!

> *One thing I discovered on my journey is that you can't be authentic with other people if you aren't authentic with yourself.*

Being inauthentic is the best way to keep your Goddess hidden away, as if she's an old sock stuffed behind your dresser with the forgotten dust bunnies. How you get into such an inauthentic place is often by telling yourself excuses or lies and then actually believing them. Those lies about not being good enough, being incompetent, or not deserving are my personal favorites that I used long ago.

Inauthentic behavior and chaos go hand in hand in life. It's the very best way to sabotage yourself and keep her away. Do you really want to be in a state of chaos? It's exhausting! I say it's time to get rid of all your dust bunnies of life and discover your Goddess!

Some good news about authenticity? It can also play a part in how people show up in your life too. If the space you are in is authentic and whole, you will attract more of that type of person or circumstances into your life, simply by being those things. If you are living with integrity and authenticity, then you will like what you see as you look in the mirror, what you are reflecting to the world.

We see trends changing in fashion, hair styles, color, and home decor every year. Why not start a trend in authenticity and see how people start to show up in each other's lives, as well as in their own? I'm actually hoping it will soon become contagious so that we end up with an epidemic of authenticity!

We Admire Authentic People

Two authentic women that come to my mind are Ellen and Oprah. Both amazing, generous, thoughtful, funny women who are also recognized by their first name and are very real. Even though they look different, come from different backgrounds, and had varied paths that brought them to their current positions in life, they both empower women with beautiful intention.

The positive effects that they create by helping women to love themselves are phenomenal! Oprah and Ellen are examples of when like attracts like in vibrational energies: two powerful women of integrity who have made their platforms about awareness, love, humor, and kindness. Over the years, I've enjoyed laughing, crying, and empathizing with both these hosts and their guests, while celebrating joys, triumphs, and life lessons with them.

What a difference these two Goddesses have made for millions of women of all kinds. I particularly loved a show of Ellen's when Oprah was a guest and I discovered that they were neighbors. The ladies appeared to be friends as they talked and laughed, being very real with each other. The presence of them together gave me goose bumps and a desire to have what they have: a realness that transcends all barriers as they enjoy the splendor of life while they make an amazing difference in the world. I am extremely grateful for their presence in my life.

The Secret to This Book

Authenticity is the real sense of who you are, feels true, and is easy to spot. It is also crucially important in maintaining your Goddess. Here, buried in this simple chapter, is the secret to my whole book. Ready?

> *When you own yourself 100%—your choices, your attitude, your honesty, and total way of being— your Goddess is right there! She's authentic, she's gracious, she's kind, and she's accountable without any effort!*

Get Your Goddess On!

Here's the other side of that secret: when you muck up your life with frustrations, grudges, lies, fears, and poisonous thoughts we have talked about in your avoidance zone, your Goddess will stay hidden. Period. Really. How do I know this? Anytime I talk about how we keep our Goddess buried, I'm writing about me, my life lessons, and how I continued to make some incredibly bad choices!

At one point or another in my life, I was mad at everyone, totally frustrated with relationships, blaming everyone and everything that wasn't nailed down, and handing out excuses like they were donuts on a Sunday morning. I didn't like myself, either.

Remember, I had no idea what a Goddess was, except when I saw one in a movie! (I equated all the Bond Girls to Goddesses in my mind! Halle is still my favorite!) I hadn't realized that I was at the college level of self-sabotage either. When I was younger, I was all about me and in the most inauthentic, selfish, me-me-me ways! I felt beautiful on the outside, but I was anything but beautiful on the inside.

I pretended that I was happy and everyone thought my life was amazing! It's perfect that I attracted that same kind of man to me in relationships, too, by dating shallow, unhappy men, who were also pretending. What a shocker! Thank goodness I moved on and shifted to another place.

Authentic Goddess Defining Opportunity

Words can be powerful, confusing, devastating, amazingly uplifting, and/or fun. Let's go with fun for this exercise. Word associations can be used in games and are also a helpful tool when writing. This exercise is to help you define yourself by writing down 12 words to describe your Goddess. It is done quickly, freely, and with an element of fun. Please note that nowhere in the instructions is overthinking. It took me approximately four minutes to do this and my words ended up to be astonishingly accurate for me, only tweaking two of them.

Please clear your mind, similar to meditation. Once you begin, just let as many words as possible flow and let your mind wander. The more time you spend contemplating these words, analyzing what would be best, or coming up with something cool that your girlfriends didn't have, the more you end up with something other than the real truth. Feel free to allow the words to spill out past the margins on the left side of the page and decide later which ones are the winners. Start with the list on the left side, grab a pencil, and begin with your flow of authentically true words when you are ready.

No cheating by doing a pre-list either; time yourself so this doesn't take you half a day.

The Authentic Goddess Defining Opportunity

1	1
2	2
3	3
4	4
5	5
6	6
7	7
8	8
9	9
10	10
11	11
12	12

Get Your Goddess On!

When you re-read your list on the left side out loud, did you feel the truth in the words? The winning words can be in whatever order you want them to be. If you are not satisfied that these words describe your authentic self, then tweak a few of them until you feel you have the finished list. Circle the 12 that speak to you.

Say them out loud a few times, then ink them into the list on the right. Your Goddess is now identified with twelve magnificent words. Writing your final list in pen says that you are committing to it. There is a reason that ink is required when you sign something legally binding. Commit to you and your Goddess.

In case anyone is interested in my 12-word list to describe my Goddess, see About the Author at the back of the book.

My Favorite Authenticity Examples

Now that I've given you the ins and outs of authenticity, I will share with you two of my favorite stories of discovering my authentic self! Even though I've been in the process of discovery for years, I continue to learn more about being real every day.

Ford: The Modeling Agency, Not the Car

My story starts at age 50, married and divorced twice, with two daughters and two stepsons later, which is why I have some gray hair and wrinkles. I was also at least four careers down the line, owned my own house and successful business, and felt physically a little frumpier than I was used to because Ms. Menopause was already starting to visit me regularly.

I was blown away when a Ford Model rep said they would be interested in me as an adult model. Well, blow me down and buy me an umbrella drink! What on earth could they see in me?

After the shock wore off, the comp card was put together and I started getting calls for photo shoots. Clients were actually picking me! I ended up doing many simple shoots for small catalogs, office furniture publications, a couple local runway shows, and even a billboard for a medical facility in California—and I was considered to be a success in the Midwest.

What did they see in me that made this happen so late in life? I surely felt that I had much more to offer in the looks department in my 20s, but no one approached me then. I had certainly changed on the outside thanks to children, years, and Ms. M's visits. What they wanted is what I represented, though: a middle-aged woman who was comfortably happy in her own skin and okay with aging.

I enjoyed being myself and happy to be able to say, "When's my next gig?" I had been on my healing journey of discovery for quite some time and I guess it was showing through in my way of being. I actually liked me and my own company so I was happy on the inside and the outside.

One of the other reasons I said yes to my less-than-glamorous three-year modeling career was because my 18-year-old daughter was increasingly getting more interested in modeling. I thought I would check out the territory to get an up close and personal look into this mysterious industry before she got involved.

I also thought it would be a great way to force me to stay in whatever shape I was in at that moment. Did you know that they actually put your sizes and measurements on those dang comp cards, even as an adult? Talk about keeping models accountable!

Get Your Goddess On!

Unfortunately, the client expects you to still be what your card says when you show up—and remember, when I was modeling, I was 50 to 53 years old. Yikes! At about 51 I started to rethink this little commitment when I was reminded of what was expected.
How often do we stay accountable in life? Not so much. But I had a card that said those blasted numbers on it, so I kept my accountability up to the highest level I ever have, made some money, and had fun. My inner Goddess and my comp card were keeping me authentic in a very inauthentic industry.

The Prize

You know how sometimes there has to be a prize at the end of a journey, to make it worth your while? Well, mine was the mother lode! I got picked to be on a segment of the Oprah show, one of her final countdown shows. It was the last one with Gayle, I believe it was called "The Girlfriends Show." All the models were in Hanes for Women (which by the way are very comfortable and I still wear my "parting gift" pieces from the show!).

You can spot me for two seconds in my magenta jacket as I look down and zip it up. Then again at the very end of the two-minute segment for Hanes, when I knelt down and spread my arms open wide with a big "ta-da" at the edge of the group of models—one of the producers asked me to do it to give the group some movement as they closed. All four seconds of fame—wow!—and I had gotten to promote amazing clothes for one of my mentor's last shows!

I knew when I was picked for the show that all those accountable moments of keeping those dang numbers in line were worth it. As I looked around at my fellow models, I saw real women. I saw women who were comfortable in their skin and our Goddesses were all on, happily representing Hanes and Oprah.

The people picking models knew what kind of women they were looking for and surprisingly I felt like I was supposed to be there, representing the petite end of the model spectrum. (Most of them were at least a foot taller than I was.) This was confirmation for me that my life was going in the right direction, and I was grateful for this life-affirming opportunity.

A Tale of My Trusty Blue Bathrobe

Story #2. Being authentic started to become more important to me in ways I couldn't imagine. I have been an artist all my life and have appreciated all arts, even if they weren't my chosen mediums. One day, I got a call that put my support to the test.

There was an art class that was being sponsored by a friend of mine, another patron of the arts. There were 12 people ready for a class, the guest artist was booked and arriving in two days, tuitions all paid, and the models for the second day all ready to go. Which brings us to the model for the first day, who had cancelled. I was called by one of the organizers of the class, a friend of a friend. I had done some figurative modeling with costumes for a local drawing group, would I consider it?

Oh, did I mention I was being asked to model for them in the buff? Gulp. Really? Do they realize this body produced children, went through menopause, and did it matter what I looked like now? They were expecting a 20-year-old college student on day one and I was a far cry from that. I proposed a compromise, that I would be semi-nude with my trusty bathrobe as my only friend up on the stage—darn, they took the compromise. I was in.

Ok, let's set the tone of this modeling gig. I was 53, done with my modeling contract, and had never even thought about doing anything like this. I even refused to do implied nude photos with

Get Your Goddess On!

any ads. My accountable little comp card was no longer something I needed to worry about, so I was actually close to the heaviest I had ever been—the same weight I was at full term with my first pregnancy—only I wasn't pregnant. Can you relate?
I had let myself go, was pale because it was late winter, saggy in places I had nightmares about, and since I wasn't dating anyone at the time, I hadn't shaved my legs in weeks! Do we have a clear picture? All I could say was, "What was I thinking?" (FYI, I did shave before class.)

I'll tell you what I was thinking. What an opportunity to make a difference! There were 12 students, one instructor, and four others who put the class together who were counting on me to help out because the event started in two days. And they agreed that I could have my sweet bathrobe as my buffer.

I had been given the opportunity to be their model in the name of art, a noble cause. No pictures were to be taken (another rule of mine), and I could drape as much or as little for my own comfort level. My Goddess rose to the challenge and I welcomed the chance to help them as I gloriously allowed myself to get even more comfortable in my skin, literally.

The difference I made by showing up, even outside my comfort level for those people, was immense. The difference I made for myself was priceless! I owned myself in my glorious skin, more than I had ever done before. My inner Goddess was in her glory. I felt relaxed, surprisingly comfortable, and honored being their semi-nude model.

My fears of having anyone see what I really looked like now became a faded concern. I had taken those fears and reality in both hands and said "Bring it on!" I was able to experience how it felt to finally conquer a silly old fear, and it felt magnificent!

Authentic Goddess Relationships

This event was one of my most solidifying and unexpectedly happy experiences. It confirmed my ideas about tapping into my Goddess, no matter what I looked like! Profound day. Profound experience for all of us involved in that art class, each for our own reasons. There were three other major benefits that came out of that day. One is that I got paid the monumental fee for the no-show model of $75.00. I had not even asked what I was to get paid, by the way, but I guess it must be the going rate for conquering fears. I donated the money directly to a local meals for charity event going on. How many people benefited from my fear conquering day, I will never know.

The second is that one of the major reasons I chose to say yes was because a dear girlfriend of mine was enrolled in the class. She told me that it could be cancelled and was quite disappointed with that possibility. I didn't tell her I was going to be her model until she got there—there's a true test of friendship!

The following Christmas, she gave me the beautiful picture she painted of me that day. I was touched and I felt like a gorgeous Goddess when I opened it! The pose was of me sitting, draped with fabric. She had made me look like one of those curvy, pale goddesses with draped fabric flowing all around in the art museums. All I needed was for her to add a couple cherubs floating above and I would have been on my way to those museum walls. Thank you, Elaine, for helping me visualize my true Goddess on canvas.

The third and most important byproduct from what I did that day is that I gained confidence and got closer to my Goddess inside and out, by trusting myself and being at peace with that power that helped me conquer my fears. My excess weight had nothing to do with my Goddess or loving myself. Why do we beat ourselves up by making up negative comments about our looks and natural beauty? It is totally destructive and counterproductive Goddess behavior. Stop doing it. This day also brought me closer to the realization of this book after I embraced how profound it was for me.

Am I advocating that every one of you Goddesses go out and find a way to get naked for an art class? Not necessarily—you'll have to find your own way to welcome your authentic self physically. It wasn't until I started writing this story that I realized the monumental experience that I had created. I had an epiphany that day and was never the same. Nothing was the same because I began to love myself more on that day.

> **It's amazing that some of the most important things you experience in life, things that shape who you are, are not line items that can be found on your resume.**

Five Steps to Your Goddess Authenticity

Since this is the age of wanting everything quickly and with the least amount of effort, I have put together a list of five easy steps that can help you on your path to finding your Goddess authenticity. Some of these steps have a whole chapter in this book devoted to them. Think of this as a bit of a book review with several chapters together in one, a concise instructional cheat sheet since you are now over halfway through your journey. These steps are also for all of humanity and are not at all gender specific.

1. Introspection
2. Acknowledgment
3. Forgive yourself and others
4. Authenticity
5. Realization—I Matter

1. Introspection—Looking in the Mirror (from Chapter 1)

Look into that mirror and ask the tough questions to get the truth about you. Who are you really? Do you like who you are and who you have become? What are the beliefs about you that you tell yourself? Are they true? What are the lies you tell yourself about you? Do you believe yourself when you say them? Why? What are your favorite qualities that you admire about yourself?

How would you describe yourself to someone else? Do you really know what your deepest desires are? What is your purpose in being here? Are you on your path that you feel is in your highest good? When are you most proud of yourself? What are you ashamed of? Are you happy? If not, what are you doing about it? If you are, do you celebrate it? Do you like you? Do you love you?

The purpose in asking even more questions is for you to really get to know who you are again. Most of us really had a sense of ourselves when we were young children, then we somehow lost that sense along the way to adulthood. Start to unearth all the misconceptions in your life by asking simple questions as we continue the learning and building process.

Introspection may not be easy at first, but will get easier with practice. The goal is for all of your answers to flow from your heart with the utmost of sincerity. Then you know you are on your authentic path.

2. Acknowledgment of the Biggest Things We Avoid (from Chapter 6)

What are the things, people, events, and situations that you avoid the most? Why? When did you first start avoiding them and are there similarities in any of them? What steps are you taking to clean up these particular areas of your life? Have you asked anyone for help along the way? How are the things in your avoidance zone holding you back? What are your biggest fears? What is holding you hostage?

As we travel through growth and discovery, the restraints that we have put on ourselves out of fear will only hold us back. If we speak about them, write about them, and confront them in the most peaceful, sincere way, we can work through them and then release.

If a young tree has restraints around its trunk that are never adjusted, it will never grow to be the size of a tree without restraints. If you keep these things that are holding you back as part of you—without the necessary shifts—your growth will never be what it could be. Find those restraints by asking yourself questions and bust right through every last one of them to conquer your fears and let those restraints go!

This could take time and sometimes requires help in the form of someone listening to you. A belief in yourself that you will triumph is very helpful as well. The more you release, the further and deeper you go into your avoidance zone to clean it out and the closer you get to your discovery of your Goddess authenticity.

3. Forgive Yourself and Others (from Chapter 7)

Please feel free to use the Three-Step Self-Forgiveness process to work through anything that has come up in both the previous steps. First **Acknowledge** what it is you are forgiving. Then **Own** the parts that you and the other people are responsible for. Lastly, **Release** those things completely in order to fully forgive. Then, follow through with an easy mantra: Forgive, Remember, Learn, and Move On . . . so that you avoid repeating yourself.

Forgiveness was the last of the cleansing steps and the beginning of the building steps, and it is so crucial for your Goddess relationship. If you ask yourself the questions and bring forward the fears of whatever is holding you back, you get the truth. Only with the truth can you fully release and lighten your load. This process has given me the confidence to release great amounts of stress and allow more joy to flow into my life. It is one of the most rewarding processes when done honestly and from the heart.

4. Authenticity 101—Moment of Trust (from Chapter 8)

This is when you are comfortable in your own skin. You are honest and true to yourself. Your center of power is available for you to own, love, and appreciate. You are now living with integrity and that brings great clarity and joy to your life. Authenticity enhances your choices and improves the quality of your life.

This is your moment to honestly trust yourself enough to fall in love with you, who you are, and who you represent to the world. Whatever you worked through in these first three steps has been released and allows you to see you—without fears, restraints, and blocks. You now have the freedom to breathe fully, maybe for the first time in years. Trust that you are as real as it gets and your life will flow in that same direction.

5. Realization—I Matter

Realizing that you matter in the world is a giant step. Your presence, your voice, your purpose, and in every moment your existence matters. You are important and the world is better because you are here. In fact, the world would not have been the same place without you here. Say out loud "I Matter" and own it every day, feel it to be true in every cell of your body and feel it in your heart. Love yourself and how you show up in the world.

There is no time frame and no one way to be on your path. Your dedication to the search within with these five steps will help you find the truth on your own personal timeline. Remember to breathe and smile along the way.

Melding Goddess with Relationships

When we show up in our relationships as the authentic beings that we are, amazing things happen in the most natural ways. I trust that you can and will be showing up 100% in your relationships now, hopefully feeling grounded and living in your power. When you show up like this, it says that you are committed to your relationships with your family, your friends, coworkers, the love of your life, and, of course, yourself. The most important relationship to continually develop and maintain is with yourself first.

As author and reader, we also have a relationship together. It's your choice as to how you want to be in our relationship because you and I are in this together. I already chose to be both vulnerable and confident by pouring 100% of myself into every word I wrote, every story I shared, and every one of the concepts that I chose to bring to light on this Goddess journey for you.

I committed to you before I even knew you. Now it's your choice as to how you show up on your journey and what you choose to do with this new information.

We have dozens of different kinds of relationships that we interact with daily. Our birth families, our chosen families, our life partners, husbands, wives, our children and step-children, our exes, friends, coworkers, acquaintances, and strangers all require different dynamics in each of these relationships. If you choose to close yourself off in any way, you might just miss out on wonderful people and events in life.

Are we supposed to show up for all of these relationships in the same way? Yes and no. No because we know more about some, others we have more concern about because they are family or very close to us, and a few we know little about or are simply

acquaintances. So being different is normal for some aspects of relationships.

The way we are supposed to show up the same for everyone is to be honest and respectful, to listen, to be present, and to see the other person for who they are. That's not too much to ask, is it? No. But do we do it? Not always. Not even with ourselves.

This is the simplest chapter, yet we seem to make it so complicated because most of the time we get in our own way.

> *In a perfect world, human interaction would be a beautiful process with complementary diversities among people being celebrated together. I dream of that space where we all get along with one another as we love and appreciate each other as we embrace our differences.*

My goal is to make relationships an easy topic, but there are two main things I have found to be the cause of the decline of so many relationships. Unfortunately, we also give our power away to these two things regularly.

One is the lack of trust and the other is conflict. When you engage in either of these forms of negative relationships, you give your power away immediately to whomever you have the issue with. Think about this the next time you choose to get involved in either of these negatively destructive relationship options. Hindsight has given me some help in minimizing the damages that I now share with you.

The Game of Conflict

There is a game that most of us play at one time or other that complicates even the best of relationships. This game has unwritten but hefty scorekeeping, no rules, and sometimes tears are involved for one or both parties. Another word for this game is "conflict," and some people play it like their life actually depends on it. The basis of this game is that each of the players wants to be right at all costs. The game has been played the same way ever since time existed, until now. I think it is highly overrated.

This is what I use for conflict resolution and it really works. Do it next time a conflict presents itself and fine tune the process for yourself for each event in your life.

Since 50% of the women reading this book may have experienced divorce, I'll use that as our example for simplicity sake. I think divorce is one of the definitions of conflict, isn't it? Let's look at divorce and its exhausting process to see how this game is played by the pros.

You and your soon-to-be ex, or already ex, are playing catch. Really imagine that the two of you are in a park, on a lawn, or at a ball field and you both have baseball gloves and just one ball. They throw it to you and you catch it. You pause and throw it back to them, kind of off to the side, so they have to work to get it. Then they throw it back to you pretty quickly, this time with increased speed, so that it burns when it hits your glove and you break a nail. You sit down and cry for a while, to ponder the pain in your hand and contemplate your next throw.

For those of you who have gone through this amazing process (I use the word amazing loosely), you know that this is exactly what a divorce looks like. Your ex sends over some simple demands, then you counter with some yeses, some nos, and add some new demands that have to be met, but haven't been discussed yet and expect cooperation.

Maybe it's property, maybe the kids, maybe the time share in Tahoe. Whatever your ball is, you know all about each other's hot spots and the issues. Insults, demands, surprises, and nastiness go back and forth, back and forth. Couples can actually play multiple versions of this same game of catch for months or years. Sound familiar? Do you really want to continue playing? Only if you are a divorce attorney.

Get Your Goddess On!

All of you that are in the 50% who haven't participated in this interesting process of divorce, insert your issue. Love relationships? Family dynamics? Estate settlements? Neighborly issues? Coworker disputes? Anything.

This game of catch very quickly becomes exhausting, debilitating, demeaning, and can guarantee stressful days and sleepless nights—especially if you are involved with more than one game of catch with multiple people at one time. Day after day, you throw, they catch, they throw, you catch—on and on. Just keeping track of all the games you've got going on could be a full-time job—too bad it doesn't pay.

Until one day, you choose to go get your nails done instead of playing catch. What would happen if you didn't catch the ball? You assessed all the costs of time, hassles, money, energy, stress, and loss of self-value and chose a different action, so you stop playing catch. What would happen?

Did you ever consider that you even had a choice to stop? Your nails would certainly look a lot better, and I'm guessing that the quality of your life would also improve. Only you can know when enough is enough.

So, imagine, they throw the ball and you duck as you get in your car and go to the salon. Since you aren't there, the ball falls to the ground. Plop. It sits there. You are in the land of acrylic and are happy to be away from the silly game. They, meanwhile, are still looking at the ground where the ball is sitting. Confusion sets in because they don't know what to do now that you're both not playing catch anymore.

You, on the other hand, are more relaxed because you are so happy to be sitting in spa land, maybe even sipping a glass of wine with cucumbers on your eyes, getting a facial with a gift certificate from your last birthday. Could this happiness possibly be your best revenge?

The other person may eventually go pick up the ball after a while and toss it in the air to themselves if they want to continue playing the game of catch, but they will soon realize that this is not as much fun, since they can't see the look on your face as it burns into your glove, or watch it go sailing over your head so you have to chase after it.

The moral of this story is that if two people are playing this game and one of them stops playing, then 2 - 1 = equals game over. This is what I like to refer to as new math.

Now, if we go back to the divorce game we used as an example, I'm sure that there is some genuine concern about who wins and who loses. Are you the weak person because you stopped playing this nasty game? No. You are the smart one. You have made a choice that the quality of your life is more important than the "ball" and are done with that game as it once existed.

If you are operating as an authentic Goddess, wouldn't you want to work things out instead? Instead of having to destroy everything in your path, at all costs, while those costs are hurting you? Yes, because even though your Goddess is power, it means *source* of power and is not interested in power struggles at any time.

So, what is next when you are done playing the game? Why not start with asking some questions of the person you are playing catch with? Can you work out a compromise? "I'll give you what you really want if you give me what I really want" kind of conversation. You won't know how close you are to resolving things unless you ask.

Considerate communication is the key to resolving the game. Maybe the other person doesn't want to play ball anymore either.

Get Your Goddess On!

What do you have to lose, except for sleepless nights, tons of billable hours, negative energy, and an inbox full of nasty emails? Is it worth it? Of course you are!

In the case of our divorce example, at a certain point you may have to do what you can, then let the attorneys play catch back and forth for a short time, and allow them to earn their lovely retainers. The attorneys sometimes will handle everything in record time when they know the game is over—I know this from experience.

The side story about the game of conflict is that the best way to win the game is to leave the ball alone and never pick it up in the first place. If we were living in an authentic, genuine, honest way, then why do we need to play that game at all anymore? What if we chose to respect each other, chose cooperation instead of conflict? What would the world be like? Game over and amazing.

A Funny Story About My Intention . . .

This is about women going through divorce. When I first got my certification as a Life Coach, I told Bob Proctor that I really wanted to work with women going through divorce to make the process easier and quicker for them. After all, I was already a bit of an expert, with two notches on my belt. (He laughed.) But, the joke was really on me.

The women I "attempted" to work with usually just wanted to blame their ex and the attorneys wanted to see how long the game would go. Heaven forbid that the divorce process would be cut short because one party was being encouraged to stop catching the ball and use cooperative communication to get it over with!

Authentic Goddess Relationships

Are you kidding? After I had invested in ads in attorney newsletters, met with many lawyers to let them know how I could help them? They generally count on all the drama, blame, and vindictiveness that both parties can muster up to stretch out all the proceedings for as long as possible. Read: billable hours = $$.

I figured this out after talking with a newly graduated attorney who accidentally told me the truth. Since my goal was to help women work through the process in the easiest way possible, no smart attorney would use my services because I would be cutting into their billable hours! Finally, an honest attorney (sort of)! This is when I was again reminded of what the real world, minus Goddess influence, really looked like.

Are You Trusting?

Lack of trust is the other destructive source that I feel affects so many people and their relationships. It can destroy them by infesting the infrastructure of a relationship, if we let it simmer under the surface. It can also involve not trusting yourself for many reasons.

Do we trust ourselves to make the best choices? Do we trust our husbands, wives, girlfriends, boyfriends, and partners? Do we trust that we are picking the right person, the right time to get married or not to get married? Do we trust we're ready to have kids? Will we ever be ready? Do I trust myself to make the best choices for everything? Why do I sometimes second guess myself?

When you first enter into any relationship—love, friendship, work/coworker, etc.—taking your time to choose someone who is trustworthy is smart. Since you have a choice as to who is in your life, wouldn't you want to choose people who you feel have the qualities you value like trust? Sometimes we don't take the time to be discerning enough and enter into various relationships on a too much, too soon basis.

This is a recipe for disaster and can lead to more continual trust issues. Sometimes we also see things that put trust in question, but choose to ignore those signs and events because we just want it to work out. Ignoring what is in front of you will almost always come back and bite you in the butt. Who's responsible for ignoring those things, then is surprised when they come to the surface? Be accountable in your relationships and keep those baby blues open to prevent those little pretend surprises.

Trust Me

My biggest question is, why did I have trust issues in the first place? When you realize you have these issues, think about what the original trigger may be. If you want the healing and moving on to be quicker and easier, focus on that first and you'll get to see who you gave your power to because they probably still have it.

I know what started it for me. Spoiler alert: another dad story. When I moved around the country as a kid, he would promise us that we would stay in the newest place, but we never did. I learned to not trust men because of it and, when he moved us one last time to a place I didn't want to go to at the tender age of 15 and a half, it all came to a head and I gave the rest of my power away to him with a great big helping of blame on the side. I really didn't know what to believe anymore.

As I got older, I wanted to continue to be right about what I believed, so of course I found men who weren't always trustworthy. Perfect! Trusting others is sometimes tricky when you really want to trust them, but you're not really sure how to. If you don't know what to trust anymore, then your life will most likely be filled with lots of ups and downs. You make choices that you don't always feel confident in . . .

Like when you go full force into that relationship without knowing too much about the person and it's not surprising that they betray you with lies or steal emotionally from you. Then you have more confirmation that you didn't really need about the lack of trust. If it's what you believe about people, though, you will continually repeat involvement with those same kind of people, over and over, until you change you and your beliefs.

One of my most prized possessions was a letter my father had written to me as he was moving us from one state to another, supposedly for the last time. (It actually ended up to be the last time.) In this letter of apology, he even promised that I could finish high school without moving again and explained how sorry he was for disappointing me once again. I was almost 16, and somehow that letter gave me a glimmer of hope that I could learn to trust him again.

Years later, I was on an airplane coming home from San Francisco and I had put my leather calendar in my carry on before I took a nap. Earlier, the man sitting next to me complimented me on its quality and took down the manufacturer's name to contact, because he really liked it. (I'll mention here that no other people were in our row.)
When I awoke, it was time for landing. I hurriedly put my magazine and water bottle into my carry on to get ready for disembarking. Since I had already put my calendar in my bag before my nap, I didn't bother to check for it. I had done my regular routine check around my seat before I got up and all was good.

Get Your Goddess On!

When I got home, after contacting the airline, I realized that the man in the next seat must have stolen my leather calendar with my precious letter tucked securely in the left front pocket. I thought it was odd that he had made a very quick exit, being less than friendly as he rushed out of the plane. Ironic that the item that had given me hope about learning to trust men again was what was stolen from me by yet another man.

Learning to Trust Again

In my stories, I've touched on the rekindled father-daughter relationship that we were able to reconstruct before he died. I think he somehow knew that trusting him was something I really wanted and needed in order to heal. We both did everything in our power to make sure our last few years together were filled with mutual respect, appreciation, love, and trust. This took work on both our parts and was done in baby steps. I also had to choose to trust him and then work at it. It was actually a beautiful process because we both wanted it.

When I eventually realized that the trust issues I developed from him were actually a combination of his issues and my issues, I was able to separate them out and it was easy to forgive and move on. I was lucky to have worked through all the important details with him before he went, because, in the end, I thankfully regained the trust I had missed for so many years. I also had to learn how to trust myself in the process. This was a valuable lesson.

Trusting yourself is so easy to say, but a little harder to execute since many of us have been so invested in some of those issues in our avoidance zone for way too long. The lack of trust was definitely a big area in my zone, but with time and realization, the pile has definitely been whittled down.

I have found that the more authentic I was with myself, the more of a natural progression it was to trust and believe in me. . . . It started with me. Then I could trust others. I started attracting very trusting and loyal people because I cleared the way for them in my life. If you are still telling yourself stories, or excuses, then it will take a little longer to trust what the woman in the mirror is saying! I give you permission to stop your stories and excuses and work through your once destructive trust issues.

Trusting 101

My favorite story of giving myself permission to authentically trust involves a stranger at an airport. We both were bellied up to one of those plug-in Wi-Fi counters at the gate, waiting to get on a connecting flight. She was obviously a service member, heading home from an assignment. We chatted briefly about her work in the military, and I thanked her for her service.

Then we talked about this and that and eventually about my latest project that I was working on called Get Your Goddess On. The entire time we chatted, a man stood across from us, looking up at us every once in a while, listening, but not acknowledging either of us.

Then, she did it. What so many women in America have probably done at least once: she packed her things up, zipped up her duffle,

looked at me and asked if I would watch her stuff while she went to the restroom. Okay, no biggie. And she was off.

The nearby man looked intently at me, then at her walking away and shrugged loudly. I looked up at him and asked, "What?" He was visibly flustered and confused as he asked me why she would ever do that, ask a total stranger to watch all her stuff. Why did she trust me?

"Don't I look trustworthy?" I asked him. I also jokingly suggested that maybe it was the innocence of my blonde curly hair (he didn't laugh) or that it was simply part of the chick thing that we do for each other, kind of like a secret sisterhood of bonding and to me it fell into the same category of women going to the bathroom in numbers. He wasn't amused—actually, he looked more disgusted.

All he said was "Women . . ." and shook his head, packed up, and got in line to board. I started literally chuckling. Of course, she would trust me—I trust me. I figured that since we had talked about both very general and personal things for about an hour, obviously, I must have given off a very authentic vibe to give her permission to trust me.

Since she was less than half my age and in a totally different pathway in life than I had been through, our life experiences didn't match up at all, but our authenticity obviously did. She was a very real person, and I appreciated that. I'm guessing she valued that in me as well. Our mutual way of being gave each other permission to trust.

I was honored to do her the favor. She had to trust me that I would do as I promised and her stuff would still be there when she got back and I had to trust that she would return. When she came back, I told her about the disgusted man across from us and we laughed. It wasn't until months later that I got the true lesson loud and clear that Brooke had taught me. Thank you.

> *Trust is a two-way street. It takes two to trust, especially in relationships.*

Because we were both being real, it worked. **Trust yourself first, and I believe you will intuitively know when it is safe to trust others.** Start by first being real, then watch to see the amazing places and people that life has in store for you on your journey.

Will there still be people that disappoint you, people you can't trust? Yes, they will still exist. Look closely at what the issue actually is, though. If it's their stuff, their trust issues, then let them keep those issues and refuse to take on their stuff and move on.

Work on your stuff. If you are continually attracting the same kind of person or situation to you, then re-examine the root of that magnet issue of trust within yourself to stop the cycle. Rework whatever is your stuff and let it go so your quality of life is improved by your efforts.

Do you have to keep those people in your life? No, not the same way you did before. Realize that you have a choice. Once they have shown themselves to be untrusting, they must earn your trust back or be cast out of your circle.

Usually when they do something once, they can do it again, so move forward with caution with these people. Be smart, but, ultimately, it's all a choice of if and how to keep them in your life. Some people do change because they want to, so give them that second chance if it's someone you value. Use your intuitive Goddess sense to guide you.

Goddess Insight

I feel that we all deserve to have several wonderfully authentic qualities in our relationships. It doesn't matter what color, gender, or race you are, or what sexual preference you have, relationships are all the same. Expect goodness and goodwill, and it will come into your life.

Get Your Goddess On!

> *I believe we all deserve love, kindness, respect, understanding, joy, and peace. What we also deserve for life in general is the ability to receive the overflowing abundance of the universe into our lives, especially in love and relationships.*

Your Goddess is actually the true you. It may not be the part you are comfortable with yet in your life, but it is the purest and most wonderful part of you! When you live in truth, your Goddess is available to you. When you can't see the truth about yourself and don't know who the real you is, it can be difficult to trust yourself at all. Start with you first.

We, as individuals, hopefully know that we matter and strive for wholeness. Before we combine ourselves into relationships with other people who may or may not be whole, always work on #1 first.

We are all just souls, beings of white light, who come here for lessons, making a difference in this world. It's our choice to be in relationships with nature, people, our work, our maker, and mostly ourselves. Your Goddess is grounded and loving. She will help you to nurture those relationships, especially with yourself if they matter to you. Trust and love you!

Chapter 8 Questions

1. Tell a story about a time when you felt genuinely authentic.

_____

_____

_____

2. What does your game of conflict look like? Who is it with and what is your ball?

Get Your Goddess On!

3. Name your top five people or situations you have trouble trusting. Then list out ways for you to work through your issues, remedy the situations, or replace what you need.

CHAPTER NINE

Get Your Power Back

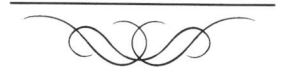

Power Literally Makes the World Go Round

Power is also our inner essence that can enhance and empower us or destroy and deplete us. Let's start with outside power and work toward the inside.

Outside power sources have been studied scientifically in many forms. Solar, nuclear, fossil fuel, electric, and wind power are sources that can all be identified, studied, and explained.

Sustainable power is a goal of many scientists as they discover new sources of power and learn new ways to protect the resources of our planet. This is the power that helps us physically function on the outside, and all of us are familiar with it. Many of these sources of power can enhance our lives in amazing ways. Power is our friend. I actually believe that some of these power sources should be listed as modern miracles.

Physically, we are all made of energy and energy is power. Our physical bodies are internally powered by the circulatory, nervous, endocrine, pulmonary, digestive, and respiratory systems, to name a few. These are all things that are also scientifically documented about our body's power system.

The inside type of power, your Goddess, is altogether different, and is not as easy to identify and explain. It's not as scientifically measured either. This power is so humbly phenomenal and is often coupled with positive intentions and healthy beliefs about ourselves. It allows us to function on a higher spiritual level, too. I believe it to be a combination of many of the concepts in this book, with a big bow of love wrapped all around it. I also feel that this inner Goddess power is a gift and should be treated with a great amount of respect.

Some people don't share my beliefs, and they interpret power negatively; it becomes dangerous and addictive when used incorrectly. In the history of the world, unnecessary religious and political wars and violent protests have happened because of this misused power. People have perished because of the destructive capabilities of it. Sometimes these byproducts make people curse, fear, or dislike power.

Hitler used this kind of power to commit unthinkable crimes against humans. John F. Kennedy used the same kind of political power for what people perceived as good. Two men in power, one hated and the other beloved. It all depended on how they used their power.

On a different, but not lesser scale, some people also use negative power in the form of "mind games" on other people to attempt to destroy their psyche. Some of these forms can look like compulsive lies, passive aggressive behavior, or verbal, emotional, or psychological abuse and many other twisted forms of torture. Even though these are not physical uses of destructive power, they can be 100% effective in destroying a person from the inside out.

Another truth about our inner power is that it can be useful, helpful, admired, valued, and also given away. Power is a form of energy within each of us that should be cherished and valued. Unfortunately, it can sometimes be underappreciated and be wasted if left "unattended" when we don't pay attention to our needs and how we are loving ourselves.

This wonderful Goddess energy is also an intuitive, loving source of power within us to help with healing and wholeness. I feel my Goddess is directly connected to my higher power and gives me a source of peace and contentment. I enjoy this abundantly spiritual yet grounded approach to life and healing. I believe this is a large part of our internal power system, but you can't physically see this kind of energy.

I have appreciated this nonphysical power source for many years and have used it with great success. After I discovered my Goddess, whenever there was a metaphoric rock, pothole, or trench in my life and I had given my power to it, knowledge followed as I regained that power. By sharing this information, my goal is to help prevent other women from giving their power away anymore. I don't know about you, but I was tired of feeling depleted because I have given too much of me away! So, I'm asking you to trust this power within you; even though you cannot see it, you can feel it inside as you heal.

A power outage in a city is easy to spot because everything goes black. A physical power outage in our bodies is also very obvious and usually looks like a heart attack or a stroke. An inner power outage can look like nothing on the outside but you can end up almost totally powerless on the inside (victim). No one would ever know anything is wrong, but there is usually great amounts of emotional pain and inner depletion associated with this type of inner power outage.

Where, Oh, Where, Did I Give My Power Away? Where, Oh, Where, Can it Be?

You know the tune of this subtitle? Have you sung this song at one time or another? Does anyone really want to feel inferior in any way, on purpose? Do you go out of your way to create events or situations where you want to end up with unfinished business? No, not usually.

The more importance you place on that event or person, though, the more you identify your life with, make excuses for, and the more power you have given to it. Unfortunately, you have also given your silent permission to become a victim at the same time. Very often it could be people in your life, but it could also be something inanimate like computers and electronics.

I was actually afraid of technology for years. I remember feeling anxious when I was first introduced to TVs with remotes, VCRs, and answering machines—anything that had an electronic component and buttons. As a child, the most technology I ever had was a 13-inch black and white TV (before remote controls), so I never grew up with any of these things. I would freeze up and ask someone else do it for me. I looked at these technology gadgets like they were from another planet.

Then came computers, printers, and cell phones, and I really went ballistic inside when I had to deal with them. My heart rate would actually increase and I would sweat like I was out in the garden on a hot day. Why, you ask? I never really took the time to understand

Get Your Power Back

technology to feel comfortable with it or appreciate it, plus there was this guy . . .

For purposes of the exercises that I ask you do in the chapters, I traced back where the worst of my fears started. There was a man in my life at the time of my initial computer experience that actually called me an idiot. (Not my dad this time.) When he saw I was having difficulties operating the basics of a computer, he would push me aside and sit down to do whatever I was attempting to do. And he would laugh at me, call me names like dumb and idiot, and make fun of how inept I was on the computer—mostly when we were alone, but sometimes in front of other people, too.

He was a real life—in my face—cyber bully and I was devastated from his verbal and emotional abuse. He would belittle me regularly. I became afraid of the computer because I thought I couldn't do it. I was also told that I would break it somehow or that I would accidentally erase everything on it. He did the same with the VCR and answering machine, also. Any questions why I felt afraid and gave my power to it? It's silly, but he and it really had a hold over me.

Why on earth would I ever tolerate that kind of behavior? This happened many, many years ago when I didn't realize what I was doing, and it was also something that I had witnessed regularly in my childhood. We've already talked about my very twisted tolerance level of abuse, but I bring it up again to show you how this kept showing up throughout every part of my life. Today, I pity anyone who would treat me that way—it would not be pretty.

To cover my inadequacies, I would even tell people jokingly that when I was in heaven, before I came down here, I had gotten in the creative gene line twice and missed the technology one. Ha Ha, people laughed, but I just felt more pain inside. I was so stupid,

Get Your Goddess On!

I couldn't figure it out, or so I had been told. Even though this treatment was a familiar experience, I never liked it, which is why I tried to cover it up with humor.

Insane that I would give my power away to this _____ (fill in the blank) man and a machine because I believed what he said. (Déjà vu with Dad.) I had given it my attention, importance, and of course my power. Triple problem. Interesting thing: when the relationship ended, my fear of computers began to subside . . .

It helped me to seek out several people in the computer world who were patient and kind in their teaching style. If someone started telling me something in the old, abusive way, I would walk away and find someone else, reinforcing my new way to learn. The fact that I wrote this book on my laptop is testament to my progress and lack of that old fear. Much lower anxiety, no sweat, go me! Now if technology would please stop advancing so fast, I think I could actually catch up!

> *We don't ever have to give any power away to anyone or anything.*

The answer was given to us a long time ago by the great Eleanor Roosevelt with those eternally profound words: "No one can make you feel inferior without your consent." I hate and love this statement. Hate it because it was available long ago and I wish I would've understood what it meant so much earlier in my life. Love it because I really get it 100% now and think she was a visionary for all people, women in particular. Men do it also, but I think women do it more often because of conditioning.

I wish I had never given my consent to spread my power to so many places, events, and people. I was beyond disappointed, mad, and disgusted with myself when it became apparent what I had done. So, all those years of blaming others were for nothing. Responsibility stings when we are learning lessons that ultimately could have been avoided. This is where I plead ignorance from not knowing I had a choice. Now I know and so do you.

Make a List

Here is a short list that I came up with in about three minutes of places and people that I have given my power away to, in no particular order. You may recognize yourself here as well:

1. Spouses and ex-spouses
2. Parents
3. Siblings
4. Employers and coworkers
5. Boyfriends/girlfriends
6. People who have criticized me
7. Mothers/fathers in law
8. Sisters/brothers in law
9. Starting a new project I'm unsure of
10. Technology and computers
11. My children
12. Insurance companies
13. Contractors at my house
14. The vacation rental company I reluctantly signed up for (don't ask)
15. Many questionable choices I'm not proud of
16. Mean girls at my four high schools
17. Other women
18. QVC
19. Money
20. Worry of the unknown

Get Your Goddess On!

I am not proud of the fact that it was so easy to have 20 power sucking things flow out so quickly. I am proud of the fact that none of them have my power today. I'm happy to say they are now all yesterday's breakfast.

Please circle all the ones on my list that are on your list, too. Write in others that are not on my list because I'm sure you have plenty of your own. Every one of these are all places to trace back to rediscover and take back your power. It's just sitting there, so now let's see how to get it back!

Life-Changing Question

You may be wondering what happened to change my scenario from "powerless bimbo victim" to "powerful amazing Goddess." The answer? Knowledge and an uncomfortable conversation with a life-changing question.

I was in my early 40s and attending a one and a half day no-name type self-help seminar in a church basement in a really small town in mid-America. I wasn't expecting much from the course because I had heard the content was a little watered down, but I was looking for answers anywhere I could find them at that point. So, when I volunteered to share my victim story in front of 50 people, I wasn't worried.

I had so many victim stories to choose from that I was still deciding which story to tell when the instructor called on me. I just knew that mine was going to be the worst in the room, as if there was some sort of worst victim story contest where the winner takes home a Jeep Wrangler. I wish.

Get Your Power Back

As I told my story of being brutally raped and beaten up, people in the room felt my pain and cried with me when I cried. I felt 100% supported. I included plenty of blame, shame, horrible details, and felt loads of sympathy from the other attendees. Then the instructor at the front of the room asked if I was done. What?

Then she looked directly at me, smirked, and asked me a life-changing question. "Do you really think this is all about you?"

Are you kidding me? Did you not hear me? Did you not feel my pain? A huge shock wave was felt all over the room. I was silent, then she asked the question again. Darn, she really expected me to answer. My voice was silent as I cried. I must have heard her wrong.

Then we started the conversation that changed my life. We went back and forth with questions and answers for each other, while my 50 new friends sat on the edge of their seats. I began to listen to her words and hate her less—maybe she had a point.

In the course of an hour and a half of standing up by the portable podium, we continued our dialog and the truth became clearer. The results of our interaction while discussing my victim story were very interesting. Here is my interpretation . . .

When the man in my story acted out horribly toward me, there must have been something really horrible inside of him to make him act out with such abusive behavior. That kind of behavior doesn't happen for no reason. Horrible pain from bad experiences, many abusive memories, low self-esteem, and huge amounts of anger were all parts of who he was inside, because that was exactly what came out of him—and it wasn't nice.

It was *his* stuff, not mine. In his actions toward me, he dumped his stuff all over me and then I made it my stuff, even though I didn't have to. I had a choice, but unfortunately chose to take on the burdens that he threw at me and I sadly believed myself to be totally worthless, again.

So, did I really give up my power to allow him, his abusive behavior, and the memories of his horrible actions to control my life and it skewed how I saw myself? Yes. Why? Because remember, I chose to believe that I somehow deserved it and then identified myself as powerless. This was totally messed up reasoning. I wish I was making it up.

So, for the cheap seats recap: for over 22 years, I gave my power away to an abusive bully who was just a damaged soul who had taken his volatile frustrations about his miserable life out on me. In a nut shell, I just got in his way. I compare it to an adult tantrum where I became his punching bag.

I also told the class about the other two women that he attacked after me, so really I was nothing special to him, just a notch on his belt of abuse. Once I finally gathered my thoughts, my analogy at the end of our conversation was a bit more upbeat.

I compared myself to a wine glass on a table in an Italian restaurant where an animated story was being told and the wine glass (me) got knocked over and broke in the middle of the story. Was it the wine glass's fault? No, it just got in the way of the person telling the story. It really had nothing at all to do with the wine glass, or me for that matter. And neither did my victim story anymore.

It really wasn't about me, it was about him and his angry stuff and I just got in the way. I looked at the instructor, then at the people in the room. I laughed a bit, then said, "I think I just wasted 22 years and I'm done with it." Just like that. I took my power back at that moment, and he has never had an ounce of it again. It's like losing 20 pounds in an instant. Very cool.

Get Your Power Back

What happened in the room in that day and a half changed more than just my life. I had worked through my biggest burden in front of 50 people with a microphone in my hand! I had volunteered to lay my life out like a Sunday brunch, and I loved how free I felt when all was said and done. The class had given me their attention, empathy, and gratitude for my willingness to be vulnerable and open up to this freeing possibility.

Two of the people who had their hands up who were not chosen came over and said that they would've caved and never gotten through it, expressing how glad they were that it was me and not them on the hot seat.

I am eternally grateful to have had the direct opportunity to heal and face every one of those fears and horrible memories in that hot seat. The whole time, I kept thinking how lucky I was that she picked me! (Well, not at first . . .) If I hadn't had to face those things, I might have never done it on my own. What a blessing!

Some other people came up and shared the profound difference that my honesty had made for them as they listened. Others told me that they had worked through their own victim stories while I was going through mine. My example of vulnerability seemed to give others permission to break through as well, and that I had helped them in some way gave me great comfort. I also felt sadness that so many other people have messed up lives, too.

Tears filled my eyes as many people told me that I had inspired them. I couldn't wrap my head around how someone like me, who had been so damaged in so many ways, could actually have inspired anyone. The pain, dedication to healing, and the willingness to be vulnerable with this group was well worth it, for all of us.

Get Your Goddess On!

I actually did get a prize afterward, in the form of about nine invitations to dinner that night. All 10 of us ate together and, one by one, told our stories and asked each other the tough questions, taking turns pretending to be the instructor.

Tears flowed and tremendous things were released as this table of 10 strangers healed together, loved together, and supported each other 100%. It changed the rest of the class for all of us because we mattered more to each other after our healing experience. Good thing the restaurant wasn't busy and we had a table in the back room.

In that course, I had raised my hand with one intention. The result of sharing my story ended up being a totally different experience for me. I just wanted that darn prize in the form of total sympathy and to be right about being a victim. What I got loud and clear was that I had been very wrong for most of my life and I was never so happy to be so wrong! There was no reason for me to stay in that victim mode. I took home two other amazing prizes as parting gifts: my freedom and I began to love myself again.

There are no accidents that I was at that particular off-beat seminar with that particular instructor, or that I raised my hand, or that she called on me, or that I shared. There is no accident that you have my journey in your hands at this very moment. The reason I was expecting and intending to get the victim of the year prize is that being a victim is what I knew how to be. Formulating a new belief about myself was the easy part in the end.

It is your choice as to what you ultimately do with your own victim story. It all becomes clearer once you take your power back, so you have the clarity you've been missing. Until then, you will remain somewhat clueless about the power in your life. The choice is yours.

Two Ways to Tell Your Story

There were two ways I told my victim story that you can see in the paragraphs above. One is that I felt I had no choice as I told my story from my familiar victim point of view, willingly giving my power away as I spoke. I felt stuck because all I had was the same answers I had told myself over and over, the same story with the same details, getting the same results. Subsequently, deeper feelings of low self-worth continued to support myself as a victim. It was a vicious cycle I felt all too comfortable in.

Then there was a shift in this chapter, when I told my story from the point of view that I was choosing to take my power back, as well as in Chapter 7, with forgiveness and my poem. Just because I had been comfortable in my victim mentality mode doesn't mean I had to stay there and continue to believe old stuff. I began the road to recovery by living my story from the view that I had now taken my power back.

Now, it's hard for me to waste 22 minutes for any reason, let alone 22 years that I can't get back. My only choice is to move forward with my knowledge and choose to keep my power. Good choice.

Five Steps to Get Your Power Back and Keep it

If you aren't happy with giving your power away to others anymore, then here are some easy steps to follow on your path to regain your power and love yourself again:

1. **Acknowledge** that you have given your power away by blaming others, allowing someone's story about you to become your personal identification, refusing to forgive yourself or others, choosing to feel inferior to someone else, being envious,

jealous, or filled with hatred; then create the desire and intention to get it back and become whole again.

2. **Identify** one category. For example, areas of life that you feel inferior in. Name your top three. Only work on one at a time and remember this is not a race or a contest. Take your time to be vulnerable, honest, and kind to yourself.

3. **Stand up** and state what you gave away, to whom, and what your goal is in getting your power back. (Examples include getting your confidence, self-worth, or freedom back.) Write all of this down in a notebook in pen so it becomes clear to you when you re-read the pages and enjoy seeing your journey unfold as you climb out of your trench.

4. Make the **conscious choice** to own that power again as you take responsibility as to how you gave it away in the first place. Use the forgiveness process to forgive your part in letting it happen. Be authentic with your intentions by being totally honest with yourself, even if you don't want to be. This process may sting at times. Just keep going.

5. Allow yourself the **possibility and probability to be whole** again as you give yourself permission to get back the power you had given away. Make the choice to love and appreciate yourself to be empowered by your own intentions and actions again. By writing these down, you can start to see a pattern in your behavior. Use this as a

preventative tool in the future. It's like coming home. Breathe. Repeat as needed.

Here is a secret: *The other person who you gave your power away to usually doesn't even know that you did it. You don't really matter to them and all this time you have inadvertently made them matter to you in the worst way, by allowing them to control you, your feelings, your emotions, and, sometimes, your behavior.*

Here is another secret: *No conversation is necessary to clear the air with them to take back your power from them. You just make the choice! They will figure it out eventually by default.*

Your actions and newly more confident behavior will say it all, without a word spoken. Enjoy your newfound freedom like the $20 bill you had all along, you just forgot that it was in your back pocket. Once you finally discard each of your issues, places, and people associated with your power losses, you will wonder why you ever made them so important in the first place. Consider this a new source of power that you have discovered. You go, Goddess!

Are you feeling empowered enough to follow through and take your power back now? Excellent! In your life party, this is the time when you feel on top of the world because you are finally enjoying your own party! Your guests are still streaming in, they are well fed, both young and old are dancing the night away, and everyone is creating positive memories. It took time, effort, and lots of planning to have such a successful event, so pat yourself on the back and appreciate yourself as a creative source of Goddess energy!

Get Your Goddess On!

Chapter 9 Questions

1. Please tell your worst victim story from the point of the view as a victim who has given her power away—the all too familiar way. Highlight all the pathetic parts where you gave your power away and are laughing at now, saying, "What was I thinking?"

2. Next, go for the gold and tell your story from an empowering point of view, as one who owns your power now. What is their stuff that you discarded? Please describe your shift.

CHAPTER TEN

The Power of Choice

You have been through a great deal of cleansing and rebuilding (and hopefully a little bit of fun) in the first nine chapters. That valuable time was for you to create a clean space and gain graceful wisdom to be able to fully love your Goddess. Let's continue the party and enjoy the fun part of this book by learning how to make new choices to get incredible results that will allow you to enjoy the remainder of your Goddess journey. The hardest part is behind you now. Celebrate!

Your rocking party is in full swing, and two of your favorite old friends just arrived, Choice and Attitude. Let's first spend some time with Choice.

Choices are not decisions—they are easier, better for you, and more powerful. Choices can be part of decisions, though.

Get Your Goddess On!

When you make a decision, usually there are a few other things that assist you to come to that particular conclusion. These are things like other people's opinions, statistics, or conditions that affect the outcome. Choices are less complicated because you only need to pick something, without any explanation. Plain and simple, they are beautiful, plentiful gifts.

I can't imagine a world without choices—let's hope we never have to see it.

When you are mindful of your choices, your results will reflect your heart. I think by looking at what you have chosen, it gives you a direct indication of where your mind has been spending time, too. Having the power to choose is a privilege. Sometimes people forget that.

I'm also going to equate making not-so-perfect choices that turn out okay after all with getting lost on vacation. Sometimes when you plan to go somewhere, you accidentally get lost on a road that takes you to a place that is absolutely breathtaking. You never would have found it if you hadn't gotten lost, and that's probably the story you will tell people when you get home.

> *My vacation postcard for you: I lost my way and then discovered another way to get back. Can't wait to tell you about this cool uncharted place I found, called a Goddess. Love, Cat*

Twelve Things I Discovered About Choices

1. Choice is the most powerful gift we have been given.

The Power of Choice

2. Who you are in the world is your choice.

3. You get to choose how you treat people, including yourself.

4. Half full or half empty is a mindset and a choice.

5. You can choose what you do for a living as many times as you want.

6. Who you love is your choice, so is how you love them.

7. Someone else has chosen to sacrifice for your freedom.

8. The choice of believing (in your Goddess) is up to you.

9. Choice is powerful, use it wisely.

10. Choices are also magical because the supply never ends.

11. Your choices can affect your attitude and your attitude can affect your choices.

12. To limit your choices is like limiting your existence.

The Real Choices within the Choices

Choices are also amazingly abundant options that can change our lives in an instant. It's time to embrace and celebrate the gift of choice every day!

Get Your Goddess On!

Many of them are on automatic and can also be referred to as habits. Some choices can be wonderfully easy and others, amazingly difficult. Do you realize how many simple choices we make every morning without even thinking, before we start our day? For example:

1. What time do I get up? Or, do I hit the snooze button and sleep in?

2. Do I exercise before breakfast, at lunch, or in the evening? Or, do I just veg on the couch?

3. Is it best to take a shower in the morning? Or, do I take a shower the night before?

4. I wonder if I should wear a suit today. Or, go with a funky ruffle blouse and a pencil skirt?

5. Socks or Hose? Flats, running shoes, sandals, or sassy heels to flaunt my calves?

6. Hair up or down? Natural curls or straightened?

These are easy. Every one of these simple choices are usually completed before you get to work. Then of course, there are even more choices as to how you get to work, once you get to work, after work, and all evening. There are literally thousands of choices we make every day, most we take for granted and don't even think about making.

There are also the more complicated kinds of choices that we deal with every day that are more introspective and require your participation. Here are some examples:

1. Do I let the ladies at work know that I'm looking for another job? Or wait till I find a better position?

2. Should I tell Carolyn her boyfriend was flirting with me in the elevator this morning? Or let it go?

3. Is it smarter to continue to make a decent living in a career that is a dead end? Or start a business doing what I'm passionate about and take a substantial pay cut?

4. Do I stay with Steve, who I've been dating for three years, but feel stale in the relationship? Or do I end that relationship and pursue a gentleman I met recently at an art gallery opening, who lives nearby?

The first list was slam dunk easy, whereas this second list involves a little more thought plus emotion, reasoning, and introspection. Still, they are all just choices. When we were young, our choices seemed easier. Do I paint with red or yellow first to make orange? Then in middle and high school our choices became downright dramatic! As we got into adulthood, we appear to have a little more control, but now the choices also seem to be so much more complicated—or are they?

If we break down each of the more introspective choices as to what the choice really is, it becomes clear and easier to make the choice. Let's use the second list of examples to simplify and decode what is the real choice.

1. Do I trust the other ladies at work to keep my secret about being unhappy in this position?

> 2. Since Carolyn's boyfriend flirts with every skirt he sees, does it even need to be mentioned?
>
> 3. Can I afford to do what I really want to do?
>
> 4. Am I really in love with Steve and do I want to wake up with him every morning?

This third set of breakdown choices should be easier to identify what the actual choice is within the second set. Choice becomes a complicated thing when we don't really know what we are choosing; it also creates tremendous confusion about our choices. When you break it down to the real choice within the choice, you get a clearer picture.

To further clarify the last example, Steve is really who you are making a choice about: whether you really love him and if you are okay with a stale relationship. Is that enough for you? In the first set of introspective questions, it would initially appear that you are making a choice between Steve and the other guy from the gallery, but that's not it at all, because you don't even know him or if he even remembers your name.

Mr. Gallery Man was just your trigger to instigate the questions and choices about Steve and your feelings for him—he is not really part of the actual choice. If you choose to leave Steve and you ever see this other man again, you may end up making a choice about him then, but it's not about him now. Right now, it's about the quality of a relationship you want or are willing to settle for with Steve. Getting clarity is key to helping you to make more informed and intelligent choices.

The Power of Choice

Choices Are Opportunities

Sometimes we love our choices and sometimes we don't. Choice is an amazing opportunity when you are sure of yourself. When you are not so sure, it can be an overwhelming and sometimes scary experience. Another important kind of choice is not making a choice, which is also a choice.

Sometimes the crazier the choices are, the cooler the results are. Even though some of my nonperfect choices have not always been good for me at the time of the choice, I somehow end up having a good result because of the lessons I learned. Some of us also make choices that save our lives. Driving sober is one of them.
There are many times when someone close to us makes a choice for us that we don't agree with; every person has lived through this type of choice at one time or another by being a child, having to go by what a parent chooses for them.

It appears that I made that obligatory not-agreeing-to choice when I was forced to follow my dad's career path for me instead of my own. I actually did make a choice to comply. Sadly, being too congenial is a choice. When this happens, many times there are things like resentment, frustration, and disappointment that tag along for the ride. It's the whole package.

On this great journey you have the choice to either believe there is a phenomenal power center inside you or not. There also may be things that I said along the way that you did not agree with. That's okay. It was my choice to write about my Goddess journey and your choice to agree with the information or not.

That's the beauty of choice: it's all yours! Even though I would love for you to believe everything I write, it will honestly not directly affect me if you make another choice. It will only affect you. My wish is that we simply choose to respect our differences.

Chocolate or Vanilla?

My favorite thing that my dad said to me was, "That's why they make chocolate and vanilla ice cream" to explain the idea of choice. I heard this statement about choices a thousand times growing up and I thought it was really funny, but now I find it to be a comforting way of life. It would be totally boring if all we had was vanilla—but sometimes that is exactly what I want.

I love having options, though—chocolate, rocky road, butter pecan, and peanut butter cup sometimes hit the spot, too. Choices are another thing that makes the world go around. Keep in mind that each of us is an individual with opinions and what you choose to learn and how you learn it is up to you. It is simply a choice you make.

For example, when I chose the name Goddess for my power center, I simply made a choice to call it that. I did not consult anyone to ask if it was okay, send it to a committee, or second guess if it was good enough. Goddess just seemed like a natural title for what I perceived as the most amazingly powerful space I could imagine.

Some choices take an instant and some choices take two years to make a reality—like the writing of this book. On my writing journey, I had choices as to what to include, how to describe each point I was sharing, and what writing style to use in general. It would take less time to build a whole house in the time it took me to write and rewrite this book. My author friend Michael Dow told me that "authors feel that their book is never really done, you eventually just have to stop," and now I understand.

I also made the emotional choice to include my own personal experiences and stories, as well as other people's stories, to portray my points and concepts. Someone originally told me to write about what I know—so here I am, reporting from the trenches of my life.

The Power of Choice

It is crucial for you to put your own situations into every part of this journey, details and all. Your own choices and stories help you to create your lessons as you travel on your personal Goddess path. Even though you are reading about me, make it about you. Exercise your choices and your free will in the process.

Choices We Take for Granted

The single most abundant thing we have available to us, besides oxygen, is choice! As I illustrated, we tend to make the simple, mundane life choices into automatic responses.

All the while we are racing through our days, we often fail to think about the fact that most of us can walk, talk, smell, see, hear, drive, and do several of these things at the same time! If we gave the automatic choices of breathing, blinking, and swallowing the reverence they deserve, we wouldn't probably get a darn thing done all day. But we would be in a state of gratitude more often!

We rush through them without thought because we have become numb to these thousands of gifts in the form of automatic choices each day. If we slow down to notice those little blessings, life would be richer and we'd realize that the key to choice is in its abundance.

Flowers for Me?

Sometimes when we take our ability to choose for granted, it can change how we look at things. Like getting a beautiful bouquet of flowers. If they arrived a few times a year like on Valentine's Day, an anniversary, and birthday, they would be appreciated and cherished. You'd probably even save the little cards tucked inside the bouquet because it's a special occasion.

But, what would happen if you got them every week? Would it make you appreciate them less because it would feel expected, even though it's still a really good thing? You might even start to take them for granted.

Those special occasions have not changed, but your view of the flowers that once went along with them could. (Any partner reading this book, please know we love getting flowers, so keep sending them—just not every week, so we have a chance to appreciate them.)

Flower deliveries are one thing to take for granted, but what if we also do that with our simple gifts of life like breathing, tasting, walking, talking, loving, and listening? If you choose to treat listening as a simple automatic thing, you miss a ton of valuable information that goes along with being present for other people.

Imagine all the aspects of listening that you would miss if you choose to simply hear (on automatic) instead of actively listening. By tuning out, you could lose sight of yet another fabulous state of awareness like caring about people. If you aren't going to choose to really listen, do us all a favor and please just put the ear buds in now and make it obvious you are zoning out.

Choose to Appreciate

I'm grateful that someone who doesn't even know me is willing to die to protect all my freedoms.

Okay, stepping on my soap box. We in America sometimes take a choice like freedom for granted. In the history of the world, vast numbers of people here and in other countries have had little to no choice in how to live.

The Power of Choice

So many women around the world have had little or no availability to even think about choices. They have amazing stories and lives of repression with great struggles and triumphs waiting for the world to hear. They know with absolute certainty that every ounce of freedom is a gift!

Please continue to think of freedom as a gift here in the United States and say thank you to those service men and women who maintain our freedom every day. The choice of sacrificing for our country that our military makes is unbelievable and brings tears to my eyes. It is the noblest of choices.

So is the choice to protect us on the streets of our cities and highways. Give gratitude whenever possible to support and appreciate the men and women who serve us as police officers, firefighters, first responders, and paramedics.

I use a couple of daily rituals to continually appreciate my choices like protection and freedom. When I take a deep breath, then blow it out, I say thank you several times a day. I feel so fortunate to be exactly where I am and able to honor and cherish my choices.

The other ritual is my secret support system in the Supportive Resource Chapter in the back. Find your own personal way to remind yourself of your freedoms, especially choice! . . . off soapbox.

Altered Consequences of a Cell Phone

What happens after we make a choice is equally as powerful in the form of consequences.

Once upon a time, I voluntarily chose to change cell phone carriers. No big deal. It looked like, smelled like, sounded like, and appeared like the guy behind the counter had everything under control.

Get Your Goddess On!

Then he pushed that button. And I discovered that since I didn't fully understand the concept of some cloud thing backing up my contacts, I had lost all my clients, friends, and family's numbers . . . so I sat down and cried.

Not a light cry, I mean a first teenage breakup waterworks sob fest . . . for about 20 minutes. Then, I stopped crying and took a breath, and another breath, and realized that I was still alive, still breathing, and I had been crying over numbers. Really? I smiled and it dawned on me that I just had the best cry in months, over numbers. I didn't even necessarily like numbers.

I had a choice to make at that moment. Do I? . . .

1. Continue with my pathetic pity party that was well under way, or do I . . .

2. Make a different choice and treat it like it was an honest mistake. I could start to put only key people back into my phone contacts. I chose 2— then added 3 also . . .

3. Learn how to back up my phone contacts so I can protect myself in the future.

In only a short time, I realized something bizarre: maybe this young man did me a favor? How could that possibly have been a favor?

A few months earlier, I had an accident when a spike from a Hawthorne tree on the edge of a golf course broke off in my right hand. I had an immediate, nasty blood infection because of the amazing amounts of pesticides, fertilizers, and other chemicals that are on and around a golf course.

The Power of Choice

I endured a trip to the emergency room, emergency surgery the next morning, two bags of antibiotics, plus four more rounds of antibiotics, and months of rehab to work toward getting the full use of my right hand back. That was what I had been going through for three months before my contacts got deleted. I was unable to continue the landscape portion of my business and had just turned over my clients to another landscaper days before.

In the blink of an eye, over half of my business was gone. My clients had been like family and I was having quite a hard time letting them and the business go—all of a sudden, everything was gone and the contacts being erased became a sort of a strange confirmation that I was supposed to move on in life. The timing of the events was uncanny, and it allowed me to actually think about what and who was important in my life.

Only certain people made it back into my phone (yes, some of my old clients, too)—a choice I made with all the people in my life. Having to reinvent myself in my late 50s ended up being an interesting consequence of my injury, too, because it gave me more time to write, which is what I ultimately wanted to do.

Because I was busy working full-time, I had not given myself permission to write like I wanted to. It turned out that the bizarre favor of erasing my contacts coincided with my life shift and allowed me the confirmation I was seeking to move forward. Bingo! Sweet consequences in the most unexpected way.

Using Your Consequences

Consequences can be really good, really bad, and everywhere in between. In my opinion, the real reason for consequences is so that we can think about what we are doing before we do it—assess, then proceed!

Get Your Goddess On!

If there were no consequences for anything, there would be no rules; without rules, we would have no life order; without life order, life would be chaotic. Talk to a kindergarten teacher if you don't know what I mean.

Consequences are really just results that keep us in check. Imagine how many people would drive drunk without any consequences—kill each other, damage property—the list is long. I am a firm believer that if we all thought about the consequences of our actions beforehand, we probably wouldn't do half the things we have done.

I went to high school and college in the 1970s so I definitely know what I'm talking about. My vocabulary contained, "What was I thinking?" far too often when I didn't think before I acted. There is an easy cure for it that I realized all too late. Pay attention to what the direct consequences of your actions could be before you make them.

One of the reasons businesses keep track of their results is so that they know what works and doesn't work for sales campaigns, ads, and day-to-day business in general. As soon as they see an undesired consequence/result of a particular ad campaign, they change what didn't work, so their result is positive and more product sells.

What if we ran our lives like our own personal business using monthly reports, so to speak? We would make ourselves more accountable for positive results. It could possibly stop us from continuing to go in nonproducing directions, so we could correct our mistakes sooner. I would have appreciated this method instead of the crash-and-burn learning method I was using for many years.

Unfortunately, I think all too often that people also don't think about consequences because they don't think they will get caught. One night I overheard two people at a restaurant talking about how they'd never get a DUI because they have done the drink and drive thing for years without getting caught and figured out the system. Good luck.

The same can be said for people who get away with cheating on their taxes and spouses, too. They are making a choice for themselves without really caring about what the consequences will be. Karma will not be their friend in the end.

Be honest. When I said consequence, I'm guessing that you thought of a negative thing that could happen to someone as a result of something they did—am I right? A consequence can be something positive, too, like I described when my phone contacts accidentally got erased and I could see a silver lining.

How about a woman who goes to school for 12 years to become a doctor and as a result of being first in her graduating class, her consequence (or result) is that she has the pick of the top internships in the country? Her result is a direct consequence of studying, paying attention, and working her butt off in medical school. Without the effort she put in for her future, the result could easily have been changed to far fewer internships to choose from. Our actions influence our consequences all the time.

Consequences are also our guidelines as to how our choices are working for us. Positive consequences = positive payoffs/gains. Negative consequences can = punishment or loss of something and foster low self-esteem. Either way, consequences are an absolutely necessary guideline of life, so pay attention and learn from them.

The Worst Thing that COULD Happen

I adopted a practice long ago where I asked myself, "What is the worst thing that could happen?" I would even list out the pros and cons of these consequences on paper. If I could live with the worst thing that could happen, then I would give it a shot. A result ending up in the positive column was always a bonus.

Of course, after making the list, I stacked my odds by immediately concentrating on the positive and what I really wanted the outcome to be. I made subsequent choices and followed through with planned actions to support my desired success.

I've learned a little more of what to expect realistically and, because of this, there is a big difference in how I approach many areas of my life now. Since I have two eyes, two ears, and only one mouth, hopefully my eyes and ears are wide open and my mouth is open only half of the time.

Next time you are in the middle of your own personal pity party, stop and realize the choices that you actually made to get there. If you didn't like your results, then concentrate on the choices you need to make to prevent that same result from happening. It's up to you if you want to repeat your mistakes or make different choices and get a different result. I ask you to stop wallowing and make a choice.

> *Our past choices help to create our present, and our present choices help to influence our future.*

Which Came First? Attitudes or Choices?

Attitudes have a way of verbally and nonverbally reflecting how a person feels in a particular situation. They also directly affect our choices and vice versa. We may never know which came first, the choice or the attitude, but we know they can directly influence each other.

The Power of Choice

Our attitude is the obvious underlying glue to everything in life! The way you approach a situation, how you show up in life, or how you come across to other people is so powerful. It can make all the difference in landing that job you want, or capturing the heart of the person you have longed for. Our attitude can be the deciding factor about the success or failure of any situation.

Have you ever met someone who you had heard great things about, then when you meet them, they seemed totally different because of their attitude—because of the vibe you got from them? Sometimes we don't even realize our attitude is offensive.

To illustrate this, think about the last time you spent time with a 15-year-old girl. Imagine that she was asked (read: forced) to do something so awful like clean her room, go to a family event, put a dress on when she wanted to wear jeans, or any other horrible request like babysitting her two little brothers.

Just wait for a moment for the attitude to show up! If you have no idea about this level of pain and suffering, please find a friend who has a teenage daughter with PMS. Sit back with a glass of wine or a cup of tea and watch the show. I would suggest you stay at least 10 to 15 feet away as you observe and wear an emotional hazmat suit to minimize the aftermath of the feelings of stupidity drifting in your direction.

Everything will be the parent's fault and you will discover that this dramatic young lady truly does live an unfair life. You will probably also experience some rolling eyes, a few "fines" mixed in, and hopefully there will be at least one storming out of the room with a door slam for your experience to be utterly complete.

Her choice of attitude is usually the worst way to really get what she wants, but since she knows it all, don't tell her. Also, us moms are so stupid and regularly get "OMG, mom, are you kidding me?

Get Your Goddess On!

Are you really going to wear that?" I don't know how we dressed ourselves for the last 40 years without our daughters' attitudes and opinions.

It would only make things worse if we reinforced our high levels of stupidity by mixing in small doses of logic as we try to talk to them. Good news on the horizon, though, eventually, we as moms become much smarter again as they get older! We also get to a master's level of intelligence when our daughters have their own 15-year-old daughters. Definition of payback.

On the other hand, go back 11 years to the attitude of that same girl when she was four years old, who loved everything about life. She reminded you of all things pink, as she devoured knowledge, rearranged her stuffed animals, had two tea parties, read four books, and changed her outfits twice—all before noon!

She still thought that you were the most amazing person in the world, anything is possible, and you had cool clothes, shoes, and jewelry. When you went to get her haircut, she wanted hers just like yours.

Same girl, same mom with just 11 years separating their experiences. What is the difference besides the years? Influence, choices, and the attitudes that she's learned and thinks that are acceptable for a 15-year-old girl's behavior. (Oh yeah, and hormones!) Attitudes vary for everyone, every day. This teenage or four-year-old girl can really make some pretty big ripples wherever she goes—good and bad—because of her attitude.

Other People's Attitudes

It is interesting how one person's attitude affects those around them. I used to have people in my life long ago who I regularly

The Power of Choice

felt like I had to walk on eggshells when they were present. Not anymore.

Ever sit down at a luncheon next to someone who was excessively chatty, overly happy, super negative, or noticeably depressed? The other person's attitude can really shift your attitude and actually affect the whole table's conversation and vibe. It can make the whole event either horrible or great, all because you allowed one person's attitude to run the show. Sometimes it's difficult not to.

I remember an opening day of one of the Star Wars movies and we really wanted to see it. I splurged on the giant theater so my daughter and I could lay back in the recliners, order a pizza, and really have the ultimate viewing experience for the debut. We were in our seats, ready for Nirvana, when a man and his son loudly came in and sat down next to us. The theater was sold out, so we couldn't move anywhere.

As the movie progressed, so did his loudness and his stories of the history of Star Wars as to why something was happening to who and when . . . you get the picture. It was so obnoxious and no one liked it, but no one said anything. Why? He stunk like a brewery. He had spilled his popcorn and part of his drink and did not respond at all to several stares and shhhhs that I carefully sent him. His drunken attitude and careless behavior told me plenty, and I chose not to invoke what could have been a nasty altercation, since I had to sit next to this mess for almost two hours.

We eventually saw the movie again without the extra show and loved it. It was our safety that motivated me to tolerate his attitude temporarily. Next time, however, I will get up, tell the usher and get my money back. I learned and will remember because my tolerance level is down to zero for abusive behavior like that.

Pay Attention to Attitudes

- Attitudes can be contagious.
- You can change a room full of people in an instant with your attitude.
- Your attitudes are obvious, even if you don't know it.
- Attitudes come from the inside and can be observed from the outside.
- Attitudes can be misinterpreted based on perception.
- Attitudes run the gamut of every emotion imaginable.
- The right attitude can bring great success. The wrong attitude can create failure.

Everything about us is so obvious to other people, even though we may not think they can see it. When attitudes are really obvious, it can look like a know-it-all type of condescending behavior, intolerant types of intelligence, or being a control freak.

Other times we are quieter and less obvious because we choose to be, or aren't sure of ourselves and look like we are being aloof or confused. Our attitude can encompass how we feel about something and is what the world ends up seeing, good or bad.

Attitudes can be faked, but most of the time the truth ends up still coming through as an undertone. They think we are not paying attention. Those people who hide their true feelings sometimes actually believe their fake attitudes are real, because they are so used to pretending. They wear masks, they hide, and they lie about how they feel and who they are. Unfortunately, they get really good at it, too. Eventually, their guard comes down and they are discovered most of the time.

I had a friend who was fooled by a con artist like this long ago. She unfortunately went wildly into a marriage with someone who had put on the "show of a lifetime" by pretending to be head over heels in love with her. It quickly became apparent that he was financially motivated. It was a costly lesson, but she's much smarter today because she's paying attention now. Attitudes can be deceiving, unless we pay attention to the signs.

Attitudes can also be very physical and quite obvious. People who have unusual piercings, gauges, multiple tattoos, or certain hair styles have chosen an outward attitude that may or may not be acceptable employee material at certain places of business, depending on the business.

If a woman applying for a high-end office job has obvious tattoos or unusual piercings, unless her qualifications exceeded the criteria, she may get passed over based on the limited opinion of the recruiter. But if she was applying for a job as a bartender at a biker bar, her look would probably be an asset.

On the flip side, if a woman wearing a suit with sensible heels walked in to apply at that same bar, she might be turned away because she didn't look right for the job either. Maybe she actually has a motorcycle and is a member of a women's biker's group but just wanted to impress the boss with a professional look. A mistake in this case because her attitude might be perceived as too stuffy for the job, simply by her appearance.

Your physical presence or outward physical attitude could mislead or guide people, so know your market and look, dress, and act according to what you want to portray. Every "look" has its niche and is perfect for its own environment because diversity and differences are yet another thing that makes the world go round.

Words and Vibes

Words that come out of our mouths, along with the tone, volume, and inflection, are the most obvious way we can show our attitude. This is especially true if we couple it with sarcasm, sassiness, or shyness. If we make eye contact when we converse, it says confidence about our attitude and so does our posture, habits, cleanliness, and respect level in our speech.

Other things that encompass attitude are kindness, love, compassion, empathy, and respect. Even though they aren't as obvious, it tells the world even a little bit more of where you are and how you want them to see you.

In the first minute or two of meeting someone, you can usually tell if you would like to spend any more time with them. They are sizing you up at the same time. The saying that you only have one chance to make a good first impression is spot on. This is true for dating, job interviews, curb appeal when selling houses, and for sure when meeting the in-laws!

An interesting example of seeing how obvious a person's attitude can be is with the concept of speed dating. This is where you sit down across the table from someone for only a few minutes and then next! You have just those few minutes to assess their looks, speech, eye contact, what they do, if they smell good or bad, their smile, how they dress, what their attitude is, and not much more. Next! It's like a live Snapchat.

The Power of Choice

What you are going to remember after the few minutes is probably their looks/smile, what they do for a living, and their attitude. It's the general indicator of where they are in life right now—their vibe. It is how you "get" them. And if you don't like the first impression, then you will probably not connect with them later during the mingle portion of the event.

Our attitudes sometimes walk into the room before us, like a strong perfume. Keeping your attitudes in check is the key to following through with your intention of how you want to appear to others. Use your 12 glorious Goddess words to keep your attitude aligned with yourself. Read them again to see if any need tweaking.

Workplace/Social Attitudes

Now let's imagine how the boss's attitude affects employees, or how much your attitude affects your department. We have all had experiences with bosses and coworkers who can really make waves and cause tons of problems if they have had a bad day. How about a situation where you don't even want to go to work or to an event because there is someone you want to avoid?

These scenarios can be at home, work, or committee meetings, with relatives, coworkers, friends, or neighbors. Do you also have people in your life who cannot think of a positive thing to say, or are so happy they seem fake? (I'm not sure why, but annual Christmas letters come to mind.)

How likely are you to purposely want to spend time with either of the super negative or way too positive attitudes? The extremes would not get my votes, but since most of us fall in between, we have a large pool of people we can choose to be around in our offices, organizations, and families.

Get Your Goddess On!

People can be divided into two basic categories as half full or half empty. It is usually easier to be around the half full people if that's what you are like. On the other hand, people who are in the lower vibrational energy, in the negative end of life, usually gravitate toward the negative half empty people. They would most likely be irritated to spend time at the happier end of the spectrum and vice versa.

If you choose to be in a state of joy and happiness, your attitude usually follows close behind because your choice, attitude, and intentions are all part of your way of being. We don't all choose positively because that's not where we are. We sometimes end up in the place where our choices lead us—a place of disease, a place of depression, or a place where we don't feel we have control anymore. We can feel very heavy and intervention is the key.

If you are not sure that attitudes can be changed at a moment's notice, just watch a toddler. Those immediate attitude adjustments are simply made by making a new choice to bring about the change. The trick is then to follow through, again and again.

An attitude really encompasses and affects all parts of you, both inside and out. Your attitude can allow you to feel like the Goddess you truly are or hold you back as if you don't deserve the possibility of this natural power.

Changing Your Attitude

I've been watching Dancing with the Stars for many years, appreciating the art of dance. While I am impressed with all the dancers, the competitors with disabilities blow my mind! How can they do what they do? For example, it takes an amputee an unbelievable amount of drive, stamina, and training to retrain their bodies and minds to just learn how to walk again, let alone dance!

These people amaze me each week, and I see them as dancing miracles. They are also people who have amazing attitudes to do what seems like the impossible, affecting not only their own lives, but everyone who watches them. Without that positive can-do attitude, they wouldn't be on the show. They inspire me to change my own attitude to "buck up and stop whining" because my problems seem so insignificant, as I see what they are dealing with.

I have been moved by their dedication and what seems like super human abilities. I recall tears streaming down my face as I watched Noah Galloway's dance for the most important year of his life. He was a marine who was injured at war, with two amputations—an arm just below the shoulder and a leg above the knee.

During the show, he shared his personal story and talked about the poor choices he made after his accident. He didn't like the results he was getting for himself, his life, or for his kids. Here is a cool secret that he showed us in the video package that went along with his dance:

> *We can make new choices and change our attitude!*
> *Just like that.*

When he did, he got vastly different results! The difference started with making a new choice, which triggered a new attitude, then followed by new actions, eventually creating amazing new results! It all started with a choice to get off his butt, change his attitude, and make a new life for himself! What an amazingly great example he set for his kids and for all of us watching him dance!

Lasting Lesson of Choosing a Positive Attitude

I was fortunate to have an opportunity to spend time with an older woman that had multiple sclerosis for over 20 years. She had been

Get Your Goddess On!

in a wheelchair for more than 10 years and couldn't use her arms very well. I went over to see her regularly and sometimes I'd wash, dry, and set her hair, or I'd feed her. We would watch soap operas or sappy movies, laugh together, and I'd make her a fun snack to give her caretaker/husband a break.

One day when I went over to visit, she was all excited and told me she needed to get all dolled up that day. She was doing a commercial on the radio for her husband's business later that day. We had such a fun time with her hair, makeup, clothes, and jewelry. We were caught up in the excitement, acting we like two little girls sneaking into our mother's closet and makeup kit!

When we were finished and waiting for a van to pick her up to go to the radio station, I asked her a simple question, "You said that this is for a radio commercial, but will there be a camera there for publicity?" She said, "No." Confused, I asked why she had gotten all dolled up when no one will even get to see all her beauty.

What she said made me really think. She said, "When I look good, I feel good and I know I will sound better on the radio. I'll feel it, and that's what will make a good radio commercial." That day, she taught me how much attitude can come from outside and directly affect the inside and vice versa. Even though I already said that the outside look of your Goddess is immaterial, if you choose it to be; for some people, it does make a big difference. I can remember when it was very important to me to look perfect and act perfect all the time in my 20s. Not as much anymore because I'm older now, and it just doesn't seem to be as important. Attitudes can always change, they can be so simple, yet so complex and connected to so much at the same time!

Years later when I was working from home and making cold calls for a company, I remembered what this sweet woman had said. I knew I could stay in my pajamas and bathrobe, lounging on the couch

The Power of Choice

to make those business calls, and I did some days. Those days were not as productive.

When I put on more businesslike clothes, pulled my hair up, and sat at my desk (makeup was always optional, of course), I would treat my calls differently and my attitude became more professional. I actually sounded more confident and, ultimately, I had more success. I remembered the radio commercial experience and thanked her in my heart for teaching me the lesson so graciously.

> (BIG, IMPORTANT SIDE NOTE: In my poem "The Moon," you will remember that the main reason I didn't report the rape was because his mom was very ill. This special woman who was in a wheelchair was the mother of my rapist. I chose to continue to go over to see her when I moved back home, even after that fateful weekend. Why? Because she was a sweet woman who I loved and I cherished our time together. I'm sure she looks down from heaven now and understands without a doubt why I could no longer be with her son. I am so grateful that her loving and positive attitude touched my life.)

The last thought on attitudes is from a friend of mine who recently told me the true difference between dogs and cats. Dogs have masters. Cats have servants. The difference is in the attitude.

Get Your Goddess On!

Chapter 10 Questions

1. List five choices you made that impacted your life for the better. List five choices you made that you now question and what you plan to do about them.

_____

_____

_____

_____

_____

_____

_____

_____

_____

_____

2. What is the difference you desire to create in the world? List 10 choices you can make today to get the results you want.

_____

_____

_____

_____

_____

_____

The Power of Choice

_____

_____

_____

_____

3. List five positive attitudes you have that you are proud of. List three attitudes you wish you didn't have and list dates when you plan to change them. (Hint: now is good.)

CHAPTER ELEVEN

How to Get What You Want

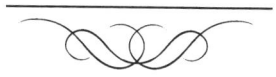

Your party is exactly what you hoped for. It was your thoughtful planning process that got you here. Everyone who came to the event will remember this time together as a night filled with magical atmosphere, delicious food, fabulous music, all-night dancing, and meaningful connections with amazing people! The most wonderful part is that you also enjoyed everything about this fun party because you prepared for it by putting only the "ingredients" together that you wanted to be here.

This also happens to be the focus of this chapter and the rest of your life. If you have sometimes gotten random results like I have, and wondered where they came from, then you will find the answers you are looking for in this chapter. And—surprise—it starts with taking responsibility!

I've already shared with you that I didn't always take responsibility of my actions. I also grew up as a parrot head, loving Jimmy

Get Your Goddess On!

Buffet's song "Margaritaville." I was comfortable with the lack of accountability the song had in the first few verses, until the disappointing end when it turns out to be "my own damn fault."

There were times when my life was really wonderful and I took full credit for creating those things. There were also times when I felt like my life tanked and those things were just happening to me because I was the victim.

Back about the time of my second divorce, my world was collapsing and uncomfortable events had been repeated in my life. I realized there was no denying it anymore. I began to think that at least a little bit was probably my own damn fault.

Unfortunately, it was more fun to stay in the denial part, so I could stay cruising on the blame boat cruise. How could I possibly have gotten a second set of these same bad results again? I didn't even want them in the first place, so why were they back? Did I ask for unworthiness and bad relationships? I must have, because that's what I got.

Learning all about the Law of Attraction in the movie The Secret didn't help my cause, either. Was I really attracting what I had in my life because I wanted it? No way! That would really suck if it were true! How could I change what was happening?

I looked for that answer on my quest of innovative ideas and concepts from leaders in the world of self-help as well as local groups in my area. I was always looking for the next great idea that could answer my question. I was drawn to some of the concepts backed with years of research, information, and examples. I was equally drawn to random ideas that also worked and just seemed to make sense. Everything in existence in our world was once simply a new idea, thought up by someone who was solving a particular problem.

Amazing things can happen when new ideas come to light, or just finding a new way of teaching old ideas can be helpful. Many times I could see how these concepts worked with other people, but I didn't fully find the answers I was looking for. I found that everything sounded pretty great in theory, though.

As I searched for answers, I discovered nuggets of knowledge in the vast amounts of wisdom of the various authors, speakers, courses, readings, and healings. These nuggets were like puzzle pieces and each one made it easier to see the whole picture and each piece fit together with another piece.

The Original Stickperson

Eventually, an idea that piqued my interest was about getting the results that I wanted while providing logical steps and simplified ways to explain my results, which is exactly what I wasn't getting. When I really looked into it, I believed it to be the answer, the place where we can get the results we actually want, by changing the way we think. I was concerned that it wasn't going to work because it seemed too easy.

In 2009, I attended a life-changing course and discovered this valuable information. I felt that I got the whole border of the puzzle all at once because it defined answers with logical steps and gave me great comfort in understanding my life. I got my huge puzzle piece when I met Bob Proctor and attended his training to become a Life Success Consultant (life coach). You may recognize his name, as he was very instrumental in helping Rhonda Byrne with the movie The Secret.

After reading the last 10 chapters, you may wonder what on earth could possibly be my qualifications to be a life coach. Here I was, a woman with an associate's degree in dental hygiene, who was a

Get Your Goddess On!

stay at home mom for over 20 years, been through two divorces, raised four kids, and who had recently had to reinvent herself at 50. What were my credentials? My hardship and bad choices? Actually, yes.

Since I had made it out, I was that woman reporting from the upper edge of the trenches that could actually understand what it's like to be there. Who better to help you out of the trouble you are in than the one who has already climbed out of the same hole others are still in?

Bob Proctor is one of the most interesting, introspective, and intuitive men I have ever met. He and his business partner Sandy Gallagher have a combined total of 75+ years of experience in speaking, writing, consulting, coaching, and mentoring to help people improve their lives, both personally and professionally. The Proctor Gallagher Institute has changed many lives, including my own. They graciously welcomed me into their Life Success Consultant family!

Before I took his course in 2009, I understood repeating mistakes like a champion. I'm sure I wrote one of the chapters in that big book of repetitive mistakes. The information Bob taught me was exactly the answer I was looking for so I could move forward in my life.

During the course, one exercise of Bob's in particular got my attention. This was a good news/bad news realization for me. It involved me being accountable for all my results, including my mistakes (darn). I got what I wanted—to find out why I kept repeating myself—and, at the same time, I had to own it (double darn). Then came the realization that just maybe I could actually do something about it. My life was never the same after that magical day that I got to spend time with two of my favorite guys, Bob and The Stickperson.

How to Get What You Want

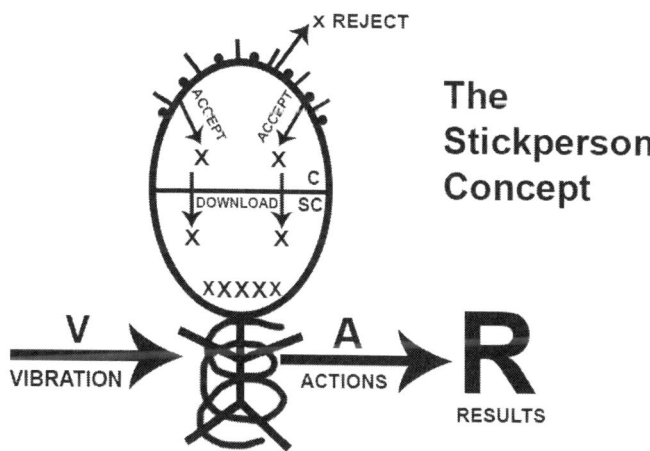

Illustration A (adapted from Concept-Therapy Institute, San Antonio, TX).

When I first saw Bob's Stickperson, he didn't look like much to me. I soon realized he was one of the best superheroes on this planet, even without a cape. The head of this guy was far larger than his body, with a line going through it horizontally. There were also five little sticks coming out of his head, and I had no idea how his tiny body, legs, and feet could support the weight of that giant head.

As you can see in illustration A, this did not look like an answer; it looked like a kid's drawing of their dad when they were in kindergarten. I seriously wondered if I made a mistake by investing in a course that used stick drawings to demonstrate a major part of their curriculum. Sure glad I was fully listening to the presentation that day Bob, because I was actually quite amazed.

There is more information on Bob Proctor and his company in the Supportive Resources chapter. Also, the movie/book *The Secret* in which he was also featured. (The original Stickperson concept was developed by one of Bob's mentors, Dr. Thurman Fleet, of the Concept-Theory Institute.)

Get Your Goddess On!

The Stick Goddess—Conscious vs. Subconscious

I thought that Bob's Stickperson needed a transformation to become a Stick Goddess for the purpose of our Goddess journey, and she is now officially part of our Goddess discovery process! This diagram is really a map of how to change your life. I'll explain first, then follow-up with a couple of very easy examples.

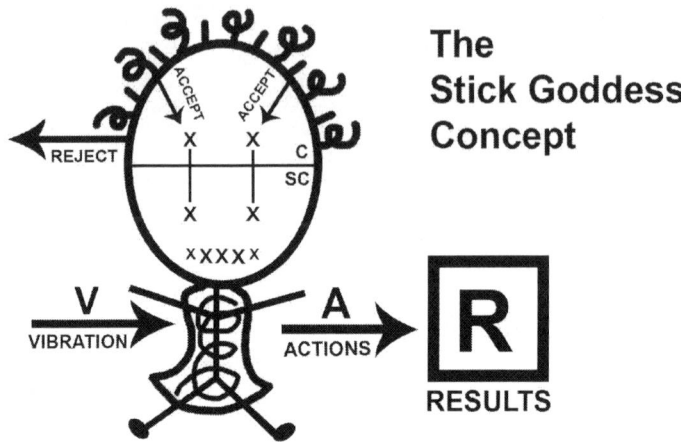

Illustration B (adapted from Concept-Therapy Institute, San Antonio, TX).

In illustration B, the top portion of the head represents the conscious mind, while the lower portion is the subconscious mind. (I believe that the avoidance zone is kept here, so be my guest and draw yours in somewhere in the lower part.) The top little five sticks on the head that look like new hair growth represent the five senses of touch, taste, smell, sight, and hearing.

The other little curls on the scalp represent the six intellectual faculties, which are imagination, intuition, memory, reasoning, perception, and will. The tiny body having a little squiggle around it is the vibrational energy; the A to the right of the body is for action and the R is your results.

Let's review what I learned during the course about the differences in our two types of minds.

1. In the conscious mind, you have the power to make a choice to accept or reject an idea, thought, or image that comes to you.

2. In the subconscious mind, you don't have the power to choose. You are on automatic. Once you have consciously chosen to accept something, it is automatically downloaded and stored in your subconscious mind as truth, like it or not.

Every conscious choice is an idea, thought, or image that goes through the accept/reject process. This is good news and bad news. Most of us would assume all conscious choices are all good because we have control of them and use free will to choose what we want. Not all of our conscious choices are in our highest good, though. (Shall we go back to my high school hideous haircut and perm choice?)

This is where I got into the most trouble: by accepting many ideas and thoughts that were not good and automatically downloaded them. They were confirmation to support my old beliefs, memories, and opinions, which were influencing my emotions, feelings, and my life. Unfortunately, they were not always in my highest good.

Since I accepted crap, it was crap that had been stored in my subconscious as crappy memories and beliefs to draw from. I got stuck in my crappy thoughts that were being stored there and then got held back by the chains of crap, which were wrapped around my crappy self. That's basically why I made the bad choices in the first place because all I was working with was crap. Got the picture?

The Stick Goddess Process Details

As we acquire ideas, thoughts, and images from the outside world, we filter them through our five senses and our six intellectual faculties. The biggest difference in these two sets of receptors is that our senses are on automatic to receive and our intellectual faculties require a bit more complicated effort, thought.

We have already talked about how we sometimes take for granted that we can see, hear, smell, taste, and touch because most of us have those on speed dial with very little conscious appreciation. For the intellectual faculties, it helps me to remember "Mr. Wipi": memory, reason, will, intuition, perception, and imagination. This second set is far more influential than we'd care to realize and, unfortunately, they all draw on what we have put in our subconscious.

- **Memory** is from our stash of past thoughts, images, events, beliefs, feelings, and ideas.

- **Reasoning** comes from the place of rational thinking and choices.

- **Will** has to do with our desire and the strength of that desire.

- **Intuition** is trusting what we feel to be true in what's right and a direction to go.

- **Perception** is about how we view things as they are, through our own filters.

- **Imagination** comes from the place where there are no limits.

1. When an idea, thought, or image comes to us from anywhere around us—any kind of outside stimulation—it is processed in either our five automatic senses or our six amazing intellectual faculties, no exceptions.

2. After we experience this outside stimulation, we go through the processing of the ideas, thoughts, and images as they arrive at the edge of our conscious mind. The problem here is that we aren't always sure what to accept and what to reject. (Hence, my bad haircut.) With experience, stored information, and by using any of the various methods of processing, we can usually make an educated choice to either accept it or not.

   If we choose to accept it, by automatically downloading it, it becomes what we base our reality on and what we believe about ourselves. Of course, if we do not choose to accept it, then it will be rejected and is gone. This is the crucial choosing process that is key to our result.

3. Once it's in the subconscious mind, it can then be stored as a memory, a belief, emotion, or feeling—positive or negative. It can also be some of the fodder that creates the sludge in our avoidance zone. It's too bad that the subconscious mind doesn't have any way to reject anything that the conscious mind sends to it.

I'd like to create a "just in case" filtering question for our mind, like we have on our computer, as a double-checking system. Do you really want to accept that? _____Accept _____Deny. Unfortunately, as its set up now, it has to accept it as true, real, and factual. Bummer. This was the key to repeating my mistakes. This was the answer I was looking for.

4. Science tells us that every single thing in life is made of energy and so are ideas, feelings, and beliefs, resonating with and through us. Based on all those thoughts about ourselves that are stored in our subconscious, our bodies follow through by creating them into real beliefs about ourselves. The vibrational energies of each of those beliefs are manifested in our bodies as truth through recognizing those vibrations (V) and what they represented.

5. With the vibrational energies aligning together with our bodies, they follow through with our physical actions (A) to stay aligned with those beliefs. This becomes who we are in the world with our actions producing the results (R) that we get in the end. These results are directly aligned with the original ideas, thoughts, and images that we accepted into our conscious mind in the first place. This is a perfect example of good in/good out or bad in/bad out.

Example #1—What Kind of Pie Do I Want to Make?

Let's pretend that I have been making the same cherry pie for years from the cherry trees in my neighbors' backyard. My cherry pies sometimes have pits (read: bumps in life) because I keep using the same recipe, same ingredients, with the same tools and the same fresh cherries. I only know how to make cherry pie one way.

One day, I get a crazy idea after I find a recipe on Pinterest that I would like to make a banana cream pie. So even though I say I want a banana cream pie, I use the same ingredients that I've always used because that's what I have available to me. What do I get? A cherry pie, not a banana cream pie. Why? Because I put in cherry pie ingredients, making no real changes.

Even though my intention was to change things up and make a new pie, I got the old one instead. How? Intentions alone aren't going to make a new pie. If I didn't do anything differently (no new action) to change the ingredients going in, I will get the same result. If you always do what you've always done, then you'll always get what you've always gotten. Cherry pie ingredients in, cherry pie out.

One day I invite my new friend, the Stick Goddess, to come over and make a pie with me. She suggests that by changing the ingredients, we can change the kind of pie we make. She says that I need to do something new and look at what I want first (the result) before I start making that pie.

We go back to the grocery store with a new list to get new ingredients! Put in something different and you get different results, she says. This is easy! So now we put in bananas instead of cherries, crumb crust instead of rolled flour crust, whipped cream on top instead of a lattice crust. Finally, we have a totally different pie by replacing the old ingredients and implementing new actions!

Get Your Goddess On!

Banana cream in, banana cream out! All we need now is two forks.

How many times did I put in more cherry pie ingredients and hope for a banana cream pie to come out? Plenty of times. This is how I've been getting the same results in my life, by doing the same things over and over, while I expected something different! I think someone said that it's also the definition of insanity. Too bad it took me so long to figure this out. This is the best shortcut ever!

So, the $64,000 question is . . . What kind of pie do you want to make now? It doesn't matter what kind of pie you made last week. The key is to look at the kind of pie you want first (results), before you begin throwing random ingredients into your pie pan.

Start your plan with a list, shop for the specific ingredients, follow the recipe, and get exactly what you expect to get. You can do this because you established your result at the beginning of the process. I know this type of process has been written about countless times, but never using pie as a most delicious method of teaching.

FYI: I was inspired to use pie as an example because I was actually writing this chapter on National Pie Day, which is March 14 (3.14) and is one of my favorite holidays all year. Eat pie and be happy is my motto!

Example #2—My Own Business

Here is another example, but this time it's a life event so you can see the specifics of how the process of accepting or rejecting the ideas can make a huge difference in real life as well!

Desired result: I want to own a successful staging and decorating business.

1. My memory provides me with the information from my father that I wasn't college material and I won't be successful unless I'm married. I reject this old idea because I know of several women who don't have degrees in decorating, some are married, some aren't, and they are all successful business owners. **Accept new idea.**

2. People I know say that I'll never make it into a new business at the age of 50. I will probably not have enough clients to make it work. Reject this idea since it doesn't support my result.

3. I search around and find places to take a course to combine my decorating talents, my organizing knowledge, my painting and landscaping skills, and my desire to work directly with people to solve their problems and sell their homes. Do the research. **Accept**

4. I take the course from stagedhomes.com and combine it with my life coach certification to be able to problem solve and listen to my clients on a higher level. **Accept** (There is more information on StagedHomes.com in The Supportive Resources chapter.)

5. I get business cards, a website, invoices, and other business materials printed, and I join a local group of stagers/realtors to mastermind the ins and outs of this new business. **Accept**

6. I go into many realtors' offices to explain the value of staging and give short presentations to get referrals. About half of them reject me and

don't want to pursue staging or any of the ideas, so I reject them for now. (Some of them called me back!) I go into many other offices that want to use me on their listings! **Accept**

7. I spend time with the offices that appreciate my work. I get an accountant to do my books and eventually have several regular offices that use me for most of their listings. I'm also doing decorating in many of the houses people are buying after I have staged their house for selling, too. Success! **Accept**

8. Now I have this wonderful situation downloaded, becoming my new truth. My vibrational energy follows through with the knowledge, experience, and the belief that I can do this and I do very well in my chosen path of decorating and staging with the supporting life coach and landscape design components in the background. Actions I take are to follow through with all my appointments, do continuing educational classes, and I end up working full-time!

9. The things, ideas, people, and thoughts that didn't support my end result were rejected immediately so I didn't have a chance to second guess myself. My old beliefs in myself based on what I was told are now all replaced with my new desired and supportive ideas, images, and thoughts.

In with the new positive ideas about myself as a successful business woman and I squash the old ones that had me questioning my abilities, being afraid of technology, and doubting that I could make it on my own. They have all been happily rejected and beautifully replaced!

10. I did this by stating my result first and believing that I could do it. Idea that I'm a smart woman enters and I **accept** it! Because I made a very thorough grocery list and stuck to it, every one of my new ingredients are ones that totally support my new desired result. I have also accepted and welcomed new and unexpected ideas, too, but they had to also be aligned with my new desired result.

    The new me is downloaded into my subconscious which is now filled with clean, clear, supportive, intelligent memories, beliefs, and reasoning. All the crap is now reduced to faded memories and nowhere to be seen! Are they still there? Yes. Do they matter? Yes, they do matter and are now serving as lessons that I choose not to repeat. Yesterday's breakfast.

11. Since you are the person making the judgment calls of what you accept and reject, you ultimately are creating your destiny with the series of choices you make. Enjoy!

Now What?

Sometimes those reinvented results, like in the case of my successful business, don't happen overnight. It took me almost five years to reap all the rewards. Of course, I had many small successes and great periods of growth and progress along the way. By keeping my eye on the result, I continued to only make choices to support success.

How much time investment are your dreams worth? It doesn't have to be years; sometimes the results I worked toward were realized before I had time to change my mind. Dreams and success need a plan. Your plan should include what you want and an idea of how to get there.

Did you know that without a target the game of darts is no fun? Start by working with one idea at a time and implement The Stick Goddess concept. Planning should also include a timeline and a list of goals for each area you are working on. The more details you can give your goals, the better.

There are many great books on the specifics of making and achieving goals. One book in particular that helped me tremendously was Train Your Brain for Success by Roger Seip. It's filled with valuable instructions, exercises, and guidelines to help you with your goals, life purpose, and timeline. If you have had difficulty with goal setting in the past, this may be a wonderful place to begin. There is contact information about Roger and his company Freedom Personal Development listed in the Supportive Resources chapter.

How Do I Start if I Don't Have a Recipe?

This is definitely not a floundering method where you see what you can come up with after you plunk a few things into a formula and get a surprise result. You start with the result you want first before you begin. It's up to you to create the look of your life, so you can then create your own recipe! You can start by listing out all the possible results you want to see happen, then pick one to start with.

How to Get What You Want

Can you imagine getting into a cab at an airport and not telling the driver where you want to go? Where would he take you? Anywhere he wants! Been there, done that, won't do that again. Only when you know the destination can you add in ideas, images, and thoughts to support that goal or desire in life (ingredients). Then map the actions that would follow through to get the results you want.

Actually write out each piece for clarity the first few times you work with your Stick Goddess. You can also alter your goal on paper if you need to. Make sure your goals are in your highest good. Allow yourself time for things to come to fruition and it will all be worth it!

I feel that the Stick Goddess is the best tool for achieving targeted results. Once the process is grasped, more than one thing can be worked on at a time, like a business and perhaps a relationship. To know how much you can handle at once, check in with your accountability because it is the key to success with your goals and results.

If you are following through on everything in one area of your life, then adding a second area is fine. If you are struggling, then wait till you are completed with your first area of focus to add anything else to your plate. Even though women are natural multitaskers, please don't make this into a competition with yourself or anyone else. Be realistic and enjoy the process! She who handles the most tasks at once doesn't necessarily win; but she is tired, irritable, and not likely to be participating in the next girls' night out!

If you ever find yourself getting stuck and perhaps not getting the results that you want, check back at what you are actually accepting and what you are believing is possible. Also check yourself to make sure you are thinking outside the box by using new and improved ingredients to get the new results you are looking for.

Get Your Goddess On!

While you are establishing your new result, plenty of people will probably put their two cents in because they are worried that you are making a mistake. When that happens, thank them for their concern, assess the value of their suggestion, and then reject the leftovers from their comments in your head, because those were old worries and may not support the newly successful picture you have in place now.

It felt so powerful when I chose to add other ideas into my conscious mind; I am confident and trust in myself and my talents: I can do it. I look back at all the years I spent repeating my mistakes and all I needed to do was come up with a new recipe with new ingredients! Too easy? No, perfect!

Chapter 11 Activity

1. Write your result first, what you want in the end.

_____

_____

_____

_____

_____

_____

_____

_____

_____

_____

How to Get What You Want

2. Write all the ideas, thoughts, and images all over the page, even if they seem silly—it can give you an interesting direction to explore.

_____
_____
_____
_____
_____
_____
_____
_____
_____
_____

3. Highlight all the ideas, images, and thoughts that you want to accept and believe.

_____
_____
_____
_____
_____
_____

Get Your Goddess On!

4. List what actions that those things will cause you to do since they are now part of you.

How to Get What You Want

5. Write out how your actions will create the results you want. What is your plan?

   _____
   _____
   _____
   _____
   _____
   _____
   _____
   _____
   _____
   _____

6. Write your result again and see how well it matches with your original goal.

   _____
   _____
   _____
   _____
   _____
   _____
   _____
   _____

CHAPTER TWELVE

Now that Your Goddess Is On

Your life party is winding down now. Most of your guests have left, some special people remain for the last few conversations of the night. You have cleaned most everything up along the way, so there is not much to do at the end. Pause and reflect on just how much fun you had during this whole process. Now that your Goddess is on, do you feel peaceful and calm? Or energetic and ready to take on the world? You are exactly where you are supposed to be as you truly begin to love yourself and your life.

Now Is Goddess Time

She is grace, love, confidence, joy, and clarity. Your newfound peace fits her well.

Working through all the stuff you have been holding onto was necessary so that you were open to receiving. If you were on overload, you first had to give some of the old stuff away before you were able to pick up something new. It also gave you a chance to see who is really under all that façade you may have been pretending to be.

Everyone starts at their own place, so whatever the beginning of your relationship with your Goddess looks like, it is exactly perfect for you. Your love and gratitude flows with ease as you reacquaint yourself with your Goddess. She is you, you are her, so enjoy the lovefest that is about to begin.

It's time to own the power we have been searching for. It's time to feel comfortable in your own skin and vow to continue to strive for personal power and excellence.

Do I have it all figured out, all the time? Heck no. I am human, and I can still make mistakes as I continue to face adversity almost daily. Nobody is perfect, and I appreciate that. What I have confidently come to know is how to trust my Goddess to help me face whatever challenges come my way. I am also comforted by our interconnectedness with every person on this planet and feel that loving connection as I ask for help and give help as needed.

What has happened on our journey together is that we went from one place to another with guidance and perseverance. As we traveled, we cleansed from many different directions, releasing things that had been stuffed away. The prize at the end is that we discovered a wonderful power within us that is destined to change our lives for the better. We also got to realize how alike we are through our similar results even though we all had different experiences. Your transformation is what you created.

The reason you were able to do this is because you showed up. It wasn't all fun and games. It took effort to clear out the years of stuff that you had forgotten was buried. But you did it. You cared enough about yourself to make that effort pay off, so that you could discover your Goddess. Be proud of your efforts.

I simply gave you suggestions based on what I learned on my journey; it was you who followed through to get your power back. Then by making new choices you ended up with a new plan and discovered a formula for getting what you want. You accomplished this by doing what you needed to do. Thank you. You are amazing.

So Now What?

Let's first assess how you feel about the changes you've made and how they feel inside. Throughout the whole process, I have asked you to look at opportunities and new ideas as possible changes for you to embrace. I realize that sometimes this can be uncomfortable, but it doesn't have to be. Change is never ending. Change is easier when you are in a good place, have a plan, and have wonderful things to look forward to.

I know it can also be scary if there are too many unknowns in the process. You now have some answers and ways of making things happen. It is very possible that if you embrace change in an empowering way, your ability to cope with change will shift and become more comfortable for you. As you continue to grow and evolve, change will be a beautiful process that you may even look forward to. Dare I hope that you will someday enjoy change as much as I do?

You now have full knowledge of this amazing place inside you that is a treasure trove filled with all the perfect power you need to access. It will always be available to help you thrive in life, no matter what direction you go in.

Get Your Goddess On!

Learning to love and grow with change is healthy because your life will never be without it. It's also important that you can count on change to be a positive influence as you look forward to new possibilities of creating an amazing future for yourself.

Maintenance Ideas

It's time to take care of you. This means unconditionally loving yourself, maybe for the first time in your life. It can be as simple as quieting yourself with deep cleansing breaths anytime you need take a moment in the midst of a hectic day. When we are quiet we can access our intuition, trust ourselves, and love every bit of us. It's all tied together.

Does being in a state of peace mean you won't have any adversity? Unfortunately not. Adversity doesn't take vacations, but we can choose how we respond to it. Disengaging is sometimes the best tactic to diffuse adversity, before it takes over.

Taking care of you involves standing up for yourself sometimes. To clarify: It is being strong, clear, kind, honest, and direct to the point, using true facts that can't be disputed. It also includes self-protection when needed.

What it isn't is a license to scream, bitch, bully, and abuse or overpower. Grace is a large part of the essence of our Goddess, so aggressive behavior is not usually part of her way of being.

Victim is another opposite of Goddess. By now, I hope it's getting easier for you to release whatever is left of any victim feelings. I urge you to move forward with the focus on embracing your power, instead of what you are releasing. Follow through with any areas that still have a hold on you so you can work through the rest of your piles of baggage.

I am proud to say that I am officially a former victim and I have both lessons and knowledge in my back pockets. When you are ready to own all of you, take all of your power back, you will someday also change your status to former.

It's too bad that so many women seem to know so much about being a victim, yet this concept of the powerful Goddess counterpart is just becoming something of interest. I'm waiting for it to become a trend for all women to live in the positive end of the spectrum.

Trust that as your Goddess gets stronger, that victim part of you will get weaker and probably go away, only to be kept as a lesson. This was my experience. I hope it will be yours.

Do one thing to empower yourself every day. Reading, journaling, looking in the mirror, standing up for yourself, breathing through adversity before you respond, loving yourself—anything that takes you in the direction of your desired results. Combine your inner power with your heart and see how fabulous life becomes.

When you're ready, address a situation where you used to feel inferior. Re-enter that space with the intention of keeping your power this time. Identify the behavior that kept you feeling powerless and do something different than your normal behavioral response. Be confident. It may not change what the other person is doing, only how you are responding to them. This is the true Goddess power.

Get the rest of your avoidance zone list out and have fun on your personal power "identify and recover" mission to all the other places to get your power back. Get your big girl panties on when you need

Get Your Goddess On!

that extra support and you go Goddess! All you need to do to get started is to do one thing in the positive direction and realize that everyone will be doing this in their own way. Ask for help when needed.

When answering a nasty text, for example, use kindness and factual words instead of whipping off a slanderous response. The conflict can be diffused with truth, kindness, and clarity. Use this technique with both texts and emails regularly for amazing results. You will feel better because it allows you to keep your power, instead of giving it away.

Chances are the other person will stop faster than you think because they no longer are getting a rise out of you with their abuse, because you stopped playing the game. It's about the control you have over your own personal power, emotions, and responses. If you do this exercise regularly, your stress should be less. Adversity will become easier as you adopt this new power protection concept and put effort toward owning your power instead of giving any more of it away. I believe that you will notice a positive, peaceful shift in yourself and in your life.

Whenever you can, acknowledge yourself doing something positive and healthy like treating yourself with respect. It's about time! The more grounded and grateful you become, the more open you will be to receiving and accepting of all the goodness, prosperity, and passion that you can possibly imagine.

It is possible that people may see a difference in you and wonder what you've been up to.

One thing you may also notice is that your intuition can be stronger, so please trust it as you discover the wonders of your Goddess transformation. Encourage your natural intuition to strengthen, by asking for it to become stronger, then trusting yourself and embracing it.

Men Benefit, Too

Thank you to the men who are reading this book. Someone obviously cares about you to have suggested it. Ladies, here is the answer to the question you have wondered all along. Yes, I wholeheartedly believe that all men can benefit from this content and it can also potentially help men find some answers to understanding women's complexities.

All men, even Chuck Norris, have a feminine side. All women, even Marilyn Monroe, have a masculine side as well. This is explained as yin and yang energy. When a man gets in touch with his feminine side, I feel that that the world is a better place—of course, I am speaking from a woman's point of view. Here's the bottom line: all men benefit from understanding their true power as well. It's time you also acknowledge your power in a non-ego way. Here is another secret just for you:

> *This book discusses things that are universal for everyone. Accountability, attitudes, choices, authenticity, avoidance, releasing, boundaries, clarity, responsibility, consequences, forgiveness, gratitude, integrity, power, clearing, trust, conflict, worthiness, and how to get what you want by changing the way you think. None of this applies only to females. This is also for you and from a woman's point of view so that, as a byproduct, you can possibly draw the insight you need to communicate with us more effectively.*

Long ago, a male friend of mine who was diagnosed with the early stages of prostate cancer took a series of female hormones as his initial treatment. His all-female staff and I were pleasantly surprised at how compassionate he was when he was on those glorious hormones! When we found out that the treatment was almost over, we joked about pooling our money together to get him another couple months of treatment. Funny but true.

So, to get in touch with your feminine side in the name of research, you don't have to go to extremes like taking female hormones, all you need to do is read. Your personal insight might arrive in ways you never expected. And think of all the points you will rack up when you can communicate more effectively with your wife/partner. Embrace your Goddess, too.

Men, if you want to conceal that you are reading this supposed "chick" book, you can put a brown paper cover on it, or simply download the e-book and no one will even know that you are reading it. Maybe it might also help you to substitute the word "Power" for "Goddess" as you read, if you choose. I would highly recommend you discussing anything and everything with the wonderful Goddess who suggested you read this book, too. Good things happen when communication improves and you end up on the same page. Enjoy!

Steps for Goddess Success

If you desire to get more out this new way of being, here are a few more organized suggestions to get started:

1. Set your intention for how you want to show up in your life. "I am_____." State things in the present and believe it's possible. Where your attention goes, energy flows. Focus on what you want and not what you don't want for this reason.

Now that Your Goddess Is On

Concentrate on your goals, dreams, and what makes your heart sing. The Law of Attraction will take care of the rest.

2. Complete the whole book, including the questions at the end of each chapter. The forgiveness exercises are key to complete your internal cleaning. Really forgive yourself most of all. Unconditionally love. Use the extra pages in the back of the book, or an extra notebook if needed, to really do the work so you feel totally released and forgiven. Embrace the gratitude of your Goddess showing up for you.

3. Read this book with a Book Club. It gives you automatic support and immediate Sister Goddesses to talk to, share ideas with, check in with, and create accountability with. Careful listening and creating a space for safe sharing are both important to build each other up. Embrace your differences.

4. Share this with all the women in your life. Share it with the men in your life, too. Ask them to read the small section addressed to men in this chapter, then download the e-book for them if they are willing. Also teach others what you have learned, because by teaching, you learn all over again.

5. Practice using the Stick Goddess for goals you set now, for projects big and small. It was actually utilized for the original concept of this book. You never know where she will take you!

6. Express your gratitude for all you have, all the special people in your life, and how your life is changing now. Show yourself some gratitude for working through this process and dedicating yourself 100%. Live in gratitude because the more you are grateful for the wonderfully abundant life you have, the more that will continue to come to you.

I am personally very grateful to you for being open to the ideas in this book and for giving them your full attention, valuable time, and effort on our journey together. Now that you have your Goddess on, I hope you're pleasantly surprised at how comfortable she feels. This is just the beginning, so expect lots more wonderful along the way. Remember to always treat yourself as if you matter, because you do.

Your Goddess is like the present you have always had hidden away, but just now discovered and opened! Cherish your precious gift as you own that power and love your life. Also, take time to support your Sister Goddesses! Experience the similarities and differences you can relate to with all these wonderful souls on the planet.

Be mindful of how connected we are to each other; also, be open to feeling the compassion and joy of this network of aliveness in just being together at this moment in time. Be there for each other in kind, thoughtful ways and see what shows up in your life! Love your Goddess, and let your love shine all over your life.

There's more to come . . . in the Supportive Resources chapter, a book club guide, and more!

CHAPTER THIRTEEN

Supportive Resources

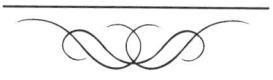

Many caring people regularly walked alongside me on my journey. They listened, advised me honestly, and suggested books, courses, and ways of thinking that were all extremely helpful. I've compiled a list of many of these sources for you to reference. Gratitude goes out to all who respected and cheered me on, as I searched for direction with hope and perseverance. Welcome, Sister Goddesses to my team of love and support.

Website: www.getyourgoddessonthebook.com
Facebook: www.facebook.com/getyourgoddessonthebook
Please like our page!
Twitter: catdolscoach
LinkedIn: www.linkedin.com/in/catdols

Get Your Goddess On!

Supportive Resources (in alphabetical order)

Abraham Hicks Publications
dailyquote@abraham-hicks.com

Bob Proctor – Proctor Gallagher Institute
www.proctorgallagherinstitute.com
Sign up for PGI Insight of the day, courses, books, and more.

Books by various authors
  The Little Soul and the Son by Neal Donald Walsh
  Conversations with God by Neal Donald Walsh
  The Power of Now by Eckhart Tolle
  A New Earth by Eckhart Tolle
  You Can't Send a Duck to Eagle School by Mac Anderson
  Think and Grow Rich by Napoleon Hill
  You Were Born Rich by Bob Proctor
  The Secret by Rhonda Byrne

Concept-Theory Institute www.concept-theory.org
Many courses available based on the teachings of Dr. Thurman Fleet. The Stickperson concept is courtesy of CTI.

doTERRA oils
Go to www.mydoterra.com/catdols for more product information. Essential oils have been extremely helpful and empowering for many aspects of my life.

Healing
  Pen Augustin www.penaugustin.com
  Pen uses multiple energy approaches to healing. She is the author of two books: Waves of Light and The Full Mood: A Priestess Tale Look for her on Twitter and Facebook, too.

  Find **Chiropractic** and **Acupuncture** offices in your area.

Supportive Resources

Reconnective Healing www.thereconnection.com to find a practitioner 1-888-374-2732 U.S.; 1-323-960-0012 Worldwide This method uses healing frequencies to bring us into alignment, balance, and harmony.

Spiritual Response Therapy Janice Puta
www.spiritual-healing-by-janice.com
janice@ourspiraljourney.com
Janice is an intuitive and a very effective teacher and consultant certified in Spiritual Response Therapy, working with you to create fulfillment, abundance, and happiness.

Jo Standing – Conquer Trauma Drama: Get Your Life Back Book and Workbook available Seven-week Resilience Program Life Resilience Coaching PTSD Resilience Facilitator

The Viva Standing Foundation supports resilience in trauma survivors nationwide both online and in person. For more information, go to www.vivastanding.org for a place of transformation and to find the answers you are looking for.
www.traumadramacoachinginstitute.com
www.traumadramaschool.com

L'Bri Pure n' Natural skin care and makeup products with aloe for healthy, beautiful skin. Go to www.catdols.lbri.com for product details.

One Divine Awakening – www.onedivineawakening.com Multiple alternative healings. This site has many healing and cleansing opportunities for you to explore. Try several.

RAINN – Rape, Abuse, and Incest National Network 1-800-656-4673 (HOPE) 24-hour hotline www.rainn.org This organization has helped 2.4 million people since 1994!

Get Your Goddess On!

Roger Seip *Train Your Brain for Success*
www. freedompersonaldevelopment.com Books, courses, and coaching on core values, purpose statement, vision statement, purpose.

StagedHomes.com – For further information on finding a stager in your area or to get more information on staging services, go to www.stagedhomes.com. Staging sells!

The Secret – by Rhonda Byrne Book and movie. www.thesecret.tv.com Several books on the Law of Attraction. Also available on Amazon.

Tapping – Emotional Freedom Technique A very simple and effective healing technique. Nick and Jessica Ortner (brother and sister team). Several books and courses available. www.thetappingsolution.com contact@thetappingsolution.com
The Tapping Solution and The Tapping Solution for Pain Relief by Nick Ortner
The Tapping Solution for Weight Management and Body Confidence by Jessica Ortner

Terri Britt – "The Worthiness Quotient" Online Quiz and six-week Worthiness Quotient training www.theworthinessquotientquiz.com Look for her on Twitter and Facebook, too.

> Author of The Enlightened Mom: *A Mother's Guide for Bringing Peace, Love and Light to Your Family's Life* – winner of Best Spiritual Book of the Year in NY and San Francisco
>
> Founder of Women Leaders of Love
> Author of the e-book, *Women Leaders of Love: How to End the #1 Massive Mistake Women Make & Unleash Your Greatest Act of Service* www.terribritt.com/leaders

Supportive Resources

Author of *Message Sent: Retrieving the Gift of Love* www.terribritt.com

Young Living Oils www.youngliving.org/catdols
Essential oils have been extremely helpful and empowering for many aspects in my life.

Cat's Positive Reminders to Live By

- Authenticity has a beautiful byproduct called joy!
- Awareness brings clarity and peace of mind.
- Be a child at heart; delay adulthood.
- Be a Goddess of Everyday Women!
- Be mindful of your choices, and your results will reflect your heart.
- Be still and listen.
- Be who you came here to be!
- Can you live with your consequences?
- Change is inevitable.
- Change is the only thing we can truly count on.
- Create your own happy ending.
- Define yourself in the world.
- Diffuse trouble with truth, kindness, and clarity.
- God gives you the grace to forgive.
- Happy accidents don't look so happy in the beginning.
- How I am in the world is my legacy.
- Know what kind of pie you are making before you start making the crust.
- Leave your ego on the sidelines.
- Let your purpose be your guideline.
- Live big; love even bigger!
- Live with integrity, love, with grace.
- Love yourself like your life depended on it! It does.
- My Goddess is my silent strength.
- Own your Power—Love your Life!

Get Your Goddess On!

- Search for truth, find yourself, your power, your Goddess!
- Find the power you left behind!
- The power of prayer trumps a royal flush every time.
- When someone throws their stuff at you, duck!
- When you're in the tough stuff, put on your "big girl panties"!
- Which came first, choices or attitudes?
- Write out wishes, embrace life, and live your dreams!
- You alone are responsible for you!
- You can't adjust your knees, but you can adjust the hem of the dress.
- You matter, I matter—Let's start acting like it!

Secret Support System

I am a spiritual woman. I believe in God and have wonderful daily conversations with my higher power to say thanks for the life I have been given. Most people would refer to this conversation as a prayer, so that's what I call it. Prayer has been used in the world for eons of time in thousands of ways and is also my secret support system.

When you remain open, the support you need is always available for you. The process of giving is two part. Imagine if you walked into a restaurant and did not ask for anything. What would the waitress bring you? Either nothing at all or anything she wanted. By asking, then being in a place of receiving, you are able to get what you ask for, or at least be in the place to find what you need. Life was not meant for you to only give to others, receiving is the other end of the giving process.

Here are two versions of this prayer, the first is for those who believe in God, beginning with Dear God. The second version is for those who may not believe in God, or who don't feel comfortable saying a prayer and begin with Dear Universe. Either way, it's all about gratitude, goodness, and your higher power, not any particular religion.

Supportive Resources

This is a blank-filled conversation that allows you to add anything you want and as much or as little as you'd like. You actually don't have to add very much for it to be complete. It's your conversation and whatever that looks like to you is perfect. It's simply a guide if you don't already have one and some possible suggestions to incorporate into your current prayers.

It can be read silently or aloud with enthusiasm. I usually read it aloud and regularly break off into another conversation about a thought, because I treat this as my time to talk directly with God. Our purpose here on Earth is to make a difference in the world—in whatever way that direction manifests for you. The quality of our journey depends on how we take care of ourselves as we are fulfilling that purpose. Start with gratitude for the things you have, then be open to receiving and see how abundant the universe becomes.

There is also a link to each prayer on the website www.getyourgoddessonthebook.com so you can download either of these prayers. Make them your own and use this as a personalized document, changing the "fill in the blank" words any time.

Be well.

Get Your Goddess On!

Dear God,
Please bless me, charge me with positive energy . . . and shower me with love and light! TY. (Thank you)

Thank you for supporting me in easily receiving love and blessings, healing, and complete balance for myself and my space—joyously, abundantly, spiritually, emotionally, mentally, physically, and financially, _____. Please help me to stay living in your presence at all times. TY.

Please do whatever is necessary to easily and quickly align the energies to be beneficial to you, to me, my life, (my) _____, _____, _____, _____, _____, _____, _____, _____, TY.

Please completely release now whatever is best for me to release, including everything and everyone I've been holding onto that is and or has been in the way of my success, especially_____ _____ _____. Please also clear and release all desire and need that I have to suffer and punish myself. Please further clear all blocks that I have to accepting love, change, and receiving goodness in my life. After releasing, please fill me with _____. My destiny is now beautifully aligned. TY.

Please continue to clear and remove from my body, mind, and spirit, whatever energies, self-limiting beliefs, misunderstandings, programing, perceptions, and judgments that no longer serve my highest good, and the good of others. Please help me to remain totally aligned with and have zero resistance to all that is in my greater good, especially _____TY.

Please God, forgive me as I forgive myself for_____ _____. I especially forgive _____.

Supportive Resources

I ask for forgiveness from_____.

I also send a message to_____ _____ saying

_____.

Please easily guide me to the next steps in my life and my relationships, and help me to recognize them, enjoy them, learn from them, and retain anything I need from the lessons, so I may continue clearly on my journey! TY.

I am so happy and grateful for (my) _____ _____ _____ _____ TY.

My present affirmations are:

I am_____, I am_____,

I am_____, I am_____,

I am_____, I am_____,

I love and accept myself. I matter! TY.

My present spiritual quality is to be_____.

I now live my life in grace through Goddess! I love and approve of myself!

Thank you, Amen

Get Your Goddess On!

Dear Universe,
Please acknowledge me, charge me with positive energy . . . and shower me with love and light! _____
_____ Thank You. (TY)

Thank you also for supporting me in easily receiving love and positive energy, healing, and complete balance for myself and my space—joyously, abundantly, emotionally, mentally, physically, and financially, _____.

Please help me to stay living at the highest vibrational level at all times. TY.
Please do whatever is necessary to easily and quickly align all energies to be beneficial to you, to me, my life, (my) _____, _____, _____, _____, _____, _____, _____, _____, TY.

Please completely release now whatever is best for me to release, including everything and everyone I've been holding onto that is and has been in the way of my success, especially _____ _____
_____. Please also clear and release all desire and need that I have to suffer and punish myself. Please also clear all blocks that I have to accepting love, change, and receiving goodness in my life. After releasing, please fill me with _____ _____. My destiny is now beautifully aligned. TY.

Please continue to clear and remove from my body, mind, and being, whatever energies, self-limiting beliefs, misunderstandings, programing, perceptions, and judgments that no longer serve my highest good or the highest good of others. Please help me to remain totally aligned with and have zero resistance to all that is in my greater good, especially _____
_____. TY.

Supportive Resources

Please Universe, forgive me as I forgive myself for

_____

I especially forgive _____

I ask for forgiveness from _____

I also send a message to _____ saying _____
_____

Please easily guide me to the next steps in my life and my relationships, helping me to recognize them, enjoy them, learn from them, and retain anything I need from the lessons, so I may continue clearly on my journey! TY.

I am so happy and grateful for (my) _____
_____ _____ TY.

I am_____, I am_____,

I am_____, I am_____,

I am_____, I am_____,

I love and accept myself. I matter. TY.

My present quality of life, is to be _____

I now live my life in grace through Goddess! I love and approve of myself!

Thank you!

Get Your Goddess On!

Goddess Glossary

We assume we know what words mean just because we have heard them and think we understand them. Here, the key words used throughout the book are defined for clarity. The space under each definition is for you to add your own if you choose. See if you can write your definitions before you read the ones already written so that it comes from the true you.

Accountable: adjective (dictionary.com)
1. Subject to obligation to report, explain, or justify something, responsible, answerable
2. Capable of being explained, explainable
3. Responsible to someone or for some actions; answerable, able to be explained (Collins English Dictionary)
4. **The sense of being responsible for your words and actions (Cat)**

Acknowledge: verb (dictionary.com)
1. To admit to be real or true; recognize the existence, truth or fact of
2. To show or express appreciation, recognition or gratitude for
3. **To make known that something or someone is real; what is (Cat)**

Attitude: noun (dictionary.com)
1. Position or posture of the body appropriate to or expressive of an action, emotion
2. The way a person views something or tends to behave toward it, often in an evaluative way
3. A position of the body indicating mood or emotion
4. **A way of verbally and nonverbally reflecting how a person feels in a particular situation (Cat)**

Supportive Resources

Authentic: adjective (dictionary.com)
1. Having the origin supported by unquestionable evidence; verified
2. Reliable; trustworthy
3. Not false or copied: genuine, real
4. Of undisputed origin: genuine (Collins English Dictionary)
5. **Being in a state of truth for every individual and genuine to oneself. This is our true soul and coincides with our true purpose for living. (Cat)**

Avoidance: noun (dictionary.com)
1. The act of voiding or keeping away from
2. Preventing from happening (Collins English Dictionary)
3. **What we don't want to deal with in our lives (Cat)**

Begin: verb (dictionary.com)
1. To come into existence; arise, originate
2. To start or cause to start (Collins English Dictionary)
3. To bring or come into being for the first time; arise or originate
4. **The very point when an idea, thought, or image becomes solidified and it starts to matter. The awakening of a new concept as it starts to become real (Cat)**

Boundary: noun (dictionary.com)
1. Something that indicates limits or limiting lines, parameter
2. Something that indicates the farthest limit, as of an area border (Collins English Dictionary)
3. **The edge of your comfort zone and the quality of life combined (Cat)**

Choice: noun/adjective (dictionary.com)
1. The right, power, or opportunity to choose
2. Something that is preferred or preferable to others; the best part of something

3. A carefully selected supply
4. Carefully selected
5. The opportunity or power of choosing (definition from Collins English Dictionary 2012)
6. **An option I pick that I want for myself or others (Cat)**

Clarity: noun (dictionary.com)
1. Clearness or lucidity as to perception or understanding; freedom from indistinctness or ambiguity
2. The state or quality of being clear or transparent to the eye
3. To be sure of and feel clear on what or who something or someone is; to know without a doubt (Cat)

Congenial: adjective (dictionary.com)
1. Agreeable/ suitable or pleasing in nature or character
2. Suited or adapted in spirit, feeling, compatible
3. Favorable, pleasant, complaisant, sympathetic
4. **The agreeable attitude that makes you go along with: when overdone, can make you powerless to do and say things you don't agree with, just to be liked (Cat)**

Consequence: noun (dictionary.com)
1. The effect, result, or outcome of something occurring earlier
2. The conclusion reached by a line of reasoning
3. An unpleasant result (definition from Collins English Dictionary 2012)
4. **This happens as a byproduct after we make a choice; used as a measurable device to see if we are going in the direction we want to be in (Cat)**

Forgive: verb (dictionary.com)
1. To grant pardon for or remission of (an offense, debt, etc.); absolve
2. To cease to feel resentment against
3. To pardon an offense or an offender.

Supportive Resources

4. To cease to blame or hold resentment against someone (Collins English dictionary)
5. **The choice to release the energy of blame toward someone or something; the result is freedom from the burden of oneself (Cat)**

Forgiveness: noun (dictionary.com)
1. The act of forgiving, the state of being forgiven
2. The disposition or willingness to forgive
3. The willingness to forgive (Collins English dictionary)
4. **The act of living in the state of forgiving (Cat)**

Goddess: noun (dictionary.com)
1. A woman of extraordinary beauty and charm
2. A greatly admired or adored woman
3. A woman who is adored or idealized, especially by a man
4. **The place in all women that is her inner power. A female with confidence in knowing who she is and how she fits into this world. This inner compass also includes love, positive energy, authenticity, accountability, kindness, and the desire to make a profound difference in life. (Cat)**

Gratitude: noun (dictionary.com)
1. The quality or feeling of being grateful or thankful
2. A feeling of thankfulness or appreciation as for gifts or favors (Collins English Dictionary)
3. **The expression of appreciation that comes from your heart to say thank you (Cat)**

Integrity: noun (dictionary.com)
1. Adherence to moral and ethical principles; soundness of moral character; honesty
2. The state of being whole, entire, or undiminished
3. A sound, unimpaired, or perfect condition

Get Your Goddess On!

4. **The drive inside a person to create the need to do the right thing and stand up for who they are in the world (Cat)**

Own: adjective (dictionary.com)
1. Of, relating to, or belonging to oneself or itself
2. To have or hold as one's own, possess
3. Belonging to oneself
4. **Responsibility for; having absolute authority of full claim of possession: It's mine! (Cat)**

Power: noun/verb/adjective (dictionary.com)
1. The ability to do or act: capability of doing or accomplishing something
2. Political or national strength, might, force; legal ability, capacity, or authority
3. The possession of control or command over others, authority ascendancy
4. To supply energy, strength; to inspire, spur, sustain
5. Operated or driven by a motor or electricity
6. **The force within us that drives who we are in the world; referred to as Goddess (Cat)**

Release: verb/noun (dictionary.com)
1. To free from confinement, bondage, obligation, pain
2. To free from anything that restrains, fastens
3. A freeing from confinement, obligation, pain, emotional strain
4. To free from captivity or imprisonment (Collins English Dictionary)
5. **To fully let go of something freely, resulting in clarity and freedom (Cat)**

Transformation: noun (dictionary.com)
1. The state of being transformed

Supportive Resources

2. Change in form, appearance, nature, or character
3. A change or alteration, especially a radical one (Collins English Dictionary)
4. **A total change as a way of being and thinking. It encompasses a person's outlook on life that alters what was to what is now, resulting in a new way of being in the world. A process that embodies inner strength, wisdom, and new possibilities. (Cat)**

Trust: noun/verb (dictionary.com)
1. Reliance on the integrity, strength, ability, surety of a person or thing
2. The obligation or responsibility imposed on a person in whom confidence or authority is placed
3. To believe
4. To permit to remain or go somewhere or to do something without fear of consequences
5. **To believe in, to expect confidence in a person or thing that there will be follow through as promised (Cat)**

Truth: noun (dictionary.com)
1. The state or character of being true
2. Actuality or actual existence
3. Honesty, integrity
4. **Actually what is, proven and factual, what we can count on to be real (Cat)**

Worthy: adjective (dictionary.com)
1. Having adequate or great merit in character; worth or value
2. Of commendable excellence or merit, deserving
3. **The level that a person is open to receive abundance from the Universe (Cat)**

Did you know that smart people always know when to ask for help? No wonder they're so smart!

CHAPTER FOURTEEN

Goddess Book Club Guide

Thank you for choosing this book for your monthly discussion! I am honored to be part of your journey in life and literature. Please feel free to share whatever you feel comfortable sharing about your Goddess experience with your group. Each of our journeys are as different as we are, so please enjoy all the points of view and learn from each other as you respect each other's boundaries.

What I suggest as you tap into your Goddess experiences is to embrace her, love her, and have fun with her in ways you may not have ever thought of before! As you share, come from your heart. Be conscious that your stories or experiences can sometimes make the most amazing difference for someone else on their journey. Welcome Sister Goddesses!

Questions and Topics for Discussion, Hopefully with Beverages and Appetizers . . .

Get Your Goddess On!

1. Do you believe in your own power? Can you relate to being called a Goddess? Why or why not? If you can't, then what would you call this power within us?

2. Which chapter/part/concept was most impactful for you and why?

3. Which chapter/part/concept did you not want to read again or deal with and why?

4. What was the most profound thing you learned about yourself in the mirror exercise?

5. Describe a time when you were way too congenial. What was the price you paid?

6. Do you feel it's more important to forgive yourself or forgive others and why?

7. As quickly as possible, go around the room and name the top five places you've given your power away to, and see if there are some common places you all can discuss. What ideas can you share to help each other to get your power back?

8. If you were given a free do-over of one event in your life, what would it be? Describe the do-over and the new outcome.

9. What is the first thing you used your Stick Goddess on and what changed when you did?

10. What is your secret support system?

11. How do you plan on showing up differently in the world now?

12. Is it easier for you to give or receive? What would you like to receive more of in your life?

Love someone today! —Cat

CHAPTER FIFTEEN

About the Author

Cat is a dog person. She's a happy-go-lucky girl next door with naturally curly hair. She's also articulate, joyful, intuitive, named after both grandmothers, creative and organized at the same time, and did I mention fun? Loving life is her passion and letting life love her back is her way of being. As a Goddess, Coach, author, and speaker, she is dedicated to helping all women discover their personal power on this journey of love and light.

She loves traveling the world whenever possible, adding stamps to her passport and sweet memories to her life. She also combines photography, gardening, and art in the form of paper making, mosaics, and hand-painted purses whenever possible because she thrives on daily doses of healthy creativity and authentic joy.

Get Your Goddess On!

Creative writing was a long-forgotten class from high school. When Cat first began this endeavor, she got lost, lost in time, lost in thought, lost in the vastness of how much to say and what to share to make the difference she dreamed of making. All she knew was that women would be her focus and empowerment was the goal.

It is fortunate that Cat discovered that her personal adversity and subsequent lessons learned were excellent training to assist other people, especially women, to take back all the power they had given away. Using humor and relatable, touching stories, Cat began helping women embrace change, making it possible for real growth and transformation.

Her wish for women is for every night to be ladies' night. Her message is to cherish all Goddess power, live in the most present way possible, and adopt this new way of being as a healthy mindset. Cat encourages sharing abundance and love with other people, enhancing life connections, and maintaining gratitude as the best underlying thread of life.

Cat's Authentic Goddess Defining Opportunity results are:

Creative	Grateful	Intuitive	Passionate
Fabulous	Grounded	Joyful	Powerful
Fun	Intelligent	Loving	Receptive

Now that you have discovered your Goddess, please share her with the world.

Be well.

NOTES AND EXTRA SPACE
FOR EXERCISES

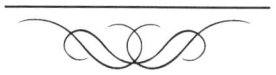

Made in the USA
Lexington, KY
17 April 2017